1295

Minds Stayed on Freedom

AUTHORS.   *Standing, back row, left to right: Kenneth Sallis, Michael Hooker, Roderick Wright, Dwyane Buchanan, Nathaniel Spurlock, Marvin Noel, Jeffrey Blackmon, John Darjean, Marques Saffold. Front row, left to right: Teleshia Kirklin, Jennifer Dixon, Willa Williams, Felisha Dixon, Tamara Wright, Lekeshia Brooks. (Not shown: Jackie Collins, Thomas Frazier, and Reginald Skinner.)*

MINDS

STAYED ON

FREEDOM

*The Civil Rights Struggle
in the Rural South,
an Oral History*

YOUTH OF THE RURAL ORGANIZING
AND CULTURAL CENTER

with an Introduction by
Jay MacLeod

Westview Press
Boulder • San Francisco • Oxford

Photograph Credits
Cover photo of Hartman Turnbow by Matt Herron, © 1978, Lorenzi–Holmes County Collection, Sojourner Archives, Washington, D.C. Text photos courtesy of the following: page ii, Dean Birkenkamp; pages 21, 35, Kenneth Sallis; page 24, Matt Herron, Lorenzi–Holmes County Collection, Sojourner Archives, Washington, D.C.; page 25, Jennifer Dixon; pages 41, 42, 79, 88, 124, 150, Sue Lorenzi, Lorenzi–Holmes County Collection, Sojourner Archives, Washington, D.C.; pages 45, 67, Marques Saffold; pages 57, 117, 143, 177, Jay MacLeod; page 81, Michael Hooker; pages 87, 96, 129, Lorenzi–Holmes County Collection, Sojourner Archives, Washington, D.C.; page 91, Jeffrey Blackmon; page 101, Nathaniel Spurlock; page 109, Felisha Dixon; page 131, Marvin Noel; page 163, Dwyane Buchanan

Published in 1991 in the United States of America by Westview Press, Inc., 5500 Central Avenue, Boulder, Colorado 80301, and in the United Kingdom by Westview Press, 36 Lonsdale Road, Summertown, Oxford OX2 7EW

Library of Congress Cataloging-in-Publication Data
Minds stayed on freedom : the civil rights struggle in the rural South
  : an oral history / the youth of the Rural Organizing and Cultural
Center ; with an introduction by Jay MacLeod.
    p. cm.
  ISBN 0-8133-1122-5—ISBN 0-8133-1123-3 (pbk.)
  1. Afro-Americans—Civil rights—Mississippi—Holmes County.
2. Civil rights movements—Mississippi—Holmes County—History—20th
century. 3. Holmes County (Miss.)—Race relations. 4. Oral
history. I. Rural Organizing and Cultural Center (Holmes County,
Miss.)
F347.H6M56 1991
305.896′0730762625—dc20   90-22134
                                                                              CIP

Printed and bound in the United States of America

The paper used in this publication meets the requirements
∞ of the American National Standard for Permanence of Paper
for Printed Library Materials Z39.48-1984.

10   9   8   7   6   5   4   3   2   1

Woke up this mornin' with my mind stayed on freedom,
Woke up this mornin' with my mind stayed on freedom,
Woke up this mornin' with my mind stayed on freedom,
Hallelu, Hallelu, Hallelujah!

—from a traditional civil rights song

Map of Holmes County, Mississippi, circa 1963

N

Cruger

HWY 49

Providence

Holly
Grove

Acona

HWY 17

Mount
Olive

Old Pilgrims
Rest

West

Tchula

HWY 12

Sunny
Mount

Long
Branch

Mileston

LEXINGTON

Second Pilgrim
Rest

Thornton

Howard
Bottom

Durant

Gages
Spring

HWY 51

Brozville

Coxburg

Shady
Grove

Ebenezer

Goodman

Pickens

CONTENTS

PREFACE

In the summer of 1989, eighteen of us eighth and ninth graders enrolled in a summer education program sponsored by the Rural Organizing and Cultural Center (ROCC). To be truthful, many of us were there because our mothers had signed us up. All of us live around Lexington, Mississippi, in Holmes County. We came to a hot and crowded classroom every morning because we knew we had a good idea: to record the experiences of Holmes Countians during the civil rights era. That's how *Minds Stayed on Freedom* began, but we never dreamt we'd become published authors.

Our main teacher was Jay MacLeod, a young man from New Hampshire who had volunteered with ROCC for two years. Willie Mae Berry, a local college student, helped teach us. But really they weren't teachers— they were guides—because we didn't learn like in school. We, the students, learned to work together and to make decisions as a group: classroom rules, what research to do, whom to interview, and everything else. We didn't mind working hard because we were in charge.

In order to know what we were doing we had to get background information. We studied interviews in other books, watched episodes of "Eyes on the Prize," examined local newspapers from 1954 to 1970 at the courthouse, and constructed a time line of civil rights events in the South and Holmes County. We soon learned to make interview guides and to listen closely to the informant so we could ask follow-up questions. We didn't want to ask yes/no questions or jerk the person around from topic to topic, so we practiced interviewing for hours and hours.

The first interview, with the Russells, was done in class so everyone could see how to do an interview. Afterwards, we used the tape to practice transcribing. In *Minds Stayed on Freedom* you will see words that seem "country," but we decided not to change the way the people we interviewed speak. We want readers to feel as though they were actually at the interview. Besides, the way our people speak is part of our culture and heritage, and we're proud of it.

Transcribing could be boring, but editing was harder. We had to cut out unimportant parts and move sections around so that the interviews flowed smoothly. That took hours and hours of work on the word processor. Some of us also did second interviews to fill in gaps from the first one. Then came writing introductions to our interviews, thinking of titles, taking photos, drawing pictures, and pasting up everything for the printer. You see, we printed *Minds Stayed on Freedom* ourselves as a magazine before Westview Press decided to make it a book. That meant more work, but we didn't mind! Now we're authors, and the other kids at school still don't believe it. We conducted two more interviews for the book and began working with Westview on the copy editing—that's editing for grammar, consistency, and style. Westview's editors had some good suggestions, but we made sure that the people's words remained the way they said them.

We regret that we could interview only fifteen people for *Minds Stayed on Freedom*. Some of our sources are our kinfolks or people we know. We also tried to get people who made important contributions to the Movement but do not get the recognition they deserve. To all those other Holmes Countians who struggled with the Movement, we salute your efforts, too.

Our title comes from a freedom song that was used to make black people in struggle unite and become stronger. That's also what happened to us as we struggled over fourteen months to make this book—we united and got stronger. We also became prouder and prouder: proud of the way our people fought for their natural rights and proud of ourselves for capturing that history for all to read and learn from.

We would like to thank all the people who helped us along the way: Ann Brown and the Rural Organizing and Cultural Center for sponsoring the project; Sally Asher for the countless hours she spent helping us to transcribe interviews, to type text into the word processor, and to lay out the final copy for the printer; and Willie Mae Berry for putting her heart into *Minds* and for putting up with us that summer. We also appreciate the help of Rayford Horton, Lynn M. Linnemeier, Amy Gutman, James "Chub" Pilgram, Sue Sojourner, and the staff of Westview Press. Thanks to *Foxfire* and *I Ain't Lying* for their example. We are especially grateful to Jay MacLeod for getting us through the tough times, for pushing us so hard to do our best, and for helping us to become a family instead of just a group of students. But most of all, we would like to express our appreciation to the people whom we interviewed. With admiration, love, and respect, we dedicate this book to your courage, determination, and spirit.

ABOUT THE BOOK
AND AUTHORS

Minds Stayed on Freedom is a vivid portrait of the civil rights struggle in one Mississippi county. While the national Movement has been painted in broad strokes by journalists and scholars, here the experiences of ordinary people bring definition to the lived texture of the Civil Rights Movement. Interviewed by local youths, Movement veterans recount how they overcame their fear in the face of terrorist resistance and collectively transformed the political and social fabric of their community. Their stories were repeated across the rural South, although seldom with the force and vigor experienced in Holmes County, located in the Mississippi plantation country.

The teenagers who conducted this oral history project strike a rare balance between poignant prose and pathbreaking research. The detailed picture that emerges from the interviews brings into sharp relief issues that remain hazy in studies of national scope: the crucial resource of black land ownership, the limited extent of church involvement, the commitment to armed self-defense, the role of women, divisions of social class within the Movement, the range of white response and retaliation, and the interplay between direct action and legal tactics.

Minds Stayed on Freedom provides plenty of fodder for academic analysis, but the interviews retain a raw, dramatic power. As project advisor Jay MacLeod of the Rural Organizing and Cultural Center writes in his introduction, "The drama in Holmes County began when a group of black farmers attempted to register to vote. Whites retaliated, pitting themselves directly against a small group of courageous black activists. The two sides battled each other. But they also battled for the hearts and minds of the black population. The tiny local Movement, armed with a vision of the future, tried to draw its people off the sidelines and into active involvement. Whites tried to keep Holmes County blacks in their 'place' with a campaign of terror and intimidation. *Minds Stayed on Freedom* tells the story of the Movement's slow, painful triumph."

As heir to the grassroots activism of the Civil Rights Movement, the Rural Organizing and Cultural Center (ROCC) is dedicated to combatting poverty and racism in Holmes County, Mississippi. ROCC developed this oral history project as part of its effort to foster pride in local history and to develop youth leadership. The authors of *Minds Stayed on Freedom* are eighth and ninth grade students, most from low-income households, who spent thousands of hours researching the local Movement, honing their questioning techniques, conducting interviews, transcribing tapes, editing their texts, and mastering the other tasks that went into the production of this book. Their success shows that ordinary people not only can make history, they also can best record it.

INTRODUCTION
Racism, Resistance, and the Origins of the Holmes County Movement

JAY MACLEOD

As the United States' most important social movement, the southern civil rights struggle has been the subject of many books. *Minds Stayed on Freedom* differs from most of the other books in two significant ways. First, it is a collection of oral histories from one of the Movement's most active battlegrounds—Holmes County, Mississippi: In this book the local people who waged the struggle are brought out of the shadows cast by national leaders and into the spotlight where they belong. Second, it is the collective achievement of young Holmes Countians who democratized the research process by converting it from a scholar's lone enterprise into an empowering learning process. The fifteen interviews conducted by these students speak to scholarly issues, but they retain the dramatic power of individual stories compellingly told. Taken together, these oral histories form a vivid tapestry of the Civil Rights Movement, which is geographically specific yet of universal interest.

This is history from below. Written history is too often that of elites: governments, statesmen, leaders. As ordinary people do not make history, so the conventional wisdom goes, it is only natural that their perspectives and contributions do not make it into history books. Howard Zinn contends that this bias in our history books hides the potential power of the masses and teaches us that "the supreme act of citizenship is to choose among saviors, by going into a voting booth every four years to choose between two white and well-off Anglo-Saxon males of inoffensive personality and orthodox opinions."[1] The Civil Rights Movement, however, is one of those heady episodes in world history that demonstrates the capacity of oppressed people to band together, to resist, and to win! Even so, the great bulk of writing on the Movement centers on national leaders and organizations, to the neglect of people at the community level who undertook the bulk of the work and endured most of the risks.

Just as Movement veterans are not mere objects of history, neither should they be mere objects of research. *Minds Stayed on Freedom* returns ownership of history to the community. The oral histories contained herein were collected by local African-American youths as part of an effort to reclaim a cultural history that is often distorted and denied. The authors were enrolled in a summer learning program sponsored by the Rural Organizing and Cultural Center (ROCC), a local, grassroots membership organization founded on the premise that community organizing and cultural heritage should reinforce each other. Because personal and collective empowerment requires an awareness of culture and history, ROCC has sponsored an essay contest on "The History of Holmes County from a Black Perspective" in the county's public schools for the past ten years. In 1988, as part of ROCC's summer education program, eighth graders produced *Bloodlines,* a seventy-page magazine based on interviews with elderly residents of the county. By forging relationships with a vanishing generation, the students recorded some of the struggles, wisdom, and folkways that make up their local cultural heritage. In the process, they acquired (almost without realizing it) a host of grammatical, compositional, editorial, and analytical skills.

In the course of exploring their history, youths become passionate learners. A lackadaisical student goes home with his taped interview and returns the next day with a forty-three page transcription, written by flashlight in the bed he shares with two cousins. Because those hours of labor were perceived as personally relevant and as a step in the creation of a tangible product, motivation was not a problem. The project pushes students to their academic limits, but instead of emphasizing their deficits, *Bloodlines* affirms the youths—their origins, their identity, and their sense of personal efficacy. Students come away inspired to embrace their future with renewed hope and vigor.

In the summer of 1989, eighteen eighth and ninth graders, half of them *Bloodlines* veterans, decided to focus on the Civil Rights Movement in *Minds Stayed on Freedom.* The students, most of whom are from low-income households, viewed the PBS documentary "Eyes on the Prize," read selections from books, and pored over old newspapers in the county courthouse. They came together for three hours each weekday morning in a sweltering classroom to hone their questioning skills, identify people to interview, and prepare their interview guides. Throughout the year, after the summer program had ended in August, the students labored during evenings and on weekends. All the tasks—transcribing tapes, editing texts, writing introductions to each piece, taking photographs, doing illustrations, researching and compiling the chronology of events, and pasting up the final copy for the printer—were undertaken by the students. They had help, but *Minds Stayed on Freedom* is their achievement.

Rather than entrust the recovery of local history to outside professionals, the Rural Organizing and Cultural Center turned historical research into a participatory learning process that enriches the community. Far from suffering, the caliber of the oral histories actually improves as a result. The questions asked and the answers given resonate with a directness, honesty, and emotion that an outside researcher could never achieve. After listening to Austry Kirklin relate the physical hardships and psychological anguish of the Jim Crow era, what scholar or journalist would come back with, "What made you all of a sudden just start the Movement? How come you didn't start it before?" That's what her two granddaughters asked, prompting an even more evocative description of African-American life prior to the civil rights struggle.

The Holmes County Movement is but one small piece of a drama that was played out across the nation. That drama drew a national audience in Montgomery, Albany, Birmingham, and Selma, but a preoccupation with the national Movement produces an incomplete picture because it fails to capture the broader base of commitment and action from which the national Movement drew its strength. An in-depth look at local Movements brings definition to important theoretical issues and sheds light on the dynamics of social change as they were experienced by the participants. To portray that lived experience in all its complexity and ambiguity—the hope, fear, faith, doubt, abandon, perseverance, and grit of Movement veterans—is the achievement of this book. Grassroots testimony from Holmes County tells us about what happened across the rural South because other local Movements drew on the same resources, confronted the same forces arrayed against them, and resisted the same internal divisions. Each community has a different story to tell, but the basic plot outline is largely shared.

The drama in Holmes County began when a group of black farmers attempted to register to vote. Whites retaliated, pitting themselves directly against a small group of courageous black activists. The two sides battled each other. But they also battled for the hearts and minds of the black population. This tiny local Movement, armed with a vision of the future, tried to draw its people off the sidelines and into active involvement. Whites tried to keep Holmes County blacks in their "place" with a campaign of terror and intimidation. *Minds Stayed on Freedom* tells the story of the Movement's slow, painful triumph.

The Holmes County Movement began in 1963; but to understand its genesis and dynamics, we must examine the county's history. As part of a ROCC project, students in a high school social-studies class mined the rich seams of that history when they produced a ninety-minute videotape entitled "Black Struggle for Equality in Holmes County, 1860–1960." Drawing on that videotape, student essays, *Bloodlines,* and other sources, this introduction seeks to contextualize the local civil rights struggle within Holmes County's larger history and within the broader Civil Rights Movement. In so doing, it delves all the way back to the county's defining institution of slavery and then traces the experiences of black Holmes Countians from the dramatic period of Reconstruction power, through the darkness of the Jim Crow period, and finally into the dawn of the civil rights era.

Holmes County

Holmes County, Mississippi, was founded in 1833 when the Choctaw Indians were deported from central Mississippi. In a mid-winter march to Oklahoma under the supervision of the U.S. government, some 14,000 Choctaws perished.[2] Of the land left behind by the Choctaws, the 820 square miles comprising Holmes County were among the most coveted by settlers and land speculators. The western quarter of Holmes County falls within the vast, flat Delta where the nation's richest soil can be found, while the rest of the county is covered with loam hills and bottom lands. Blacks have heavily outnumbered whites since slavery, but the county has always been dominated by whites—Delta planters and a business and professional elite.

African Americans in Holmes County have always resisted white domination. Even when they were bought and sold like cattle, blacks found ways through cultural resistance to defy white will and to create their own world in which human dignity and autonomy flourished. Sometimes their resistance was overt. In 1835, according to testimony collected in the 1930s, a slave revolt kindled by the white outlaw John Murrell was averted when "Vigilance Committees were organized and the negroes and white people suspected of abetting the alleged insurrection were brought before the committees of Safety and those who were found guilty were severely punished."[3]

Elvira Boles, ninety-four years old when she was interviewed in 1936, recalled her life as a slave in Holmes County.

> I'se a child of the marster. His wife, she sold me. Dey tuk us to where dere was a heap o' white people down by the coaht-house [courthouse] and we'd be there in lots and den de whites 'ud bid for us. Man bought me was Elihn Boles.
>
> I don' know how old I was, but I washed dishes at de marster's house. Den dey put me in the fields. We don' git a nickel in slavery. I worked in field and brick yard. Toted brick, six bricks each load all day. That's the reason I ain't no-count. I'se worked to death. I had to wok evva day.

I'd leave mah baby cryin' in the yard and I'd be cryin', but I couldn't stay. Done evvy thing but split rails. I've cut timber an' ah ploughed. Done evvy thing a man could do. I couldn't notice the time, but I'd be glad to get back to my baby. My oldest child, he boy by Boles, almost white.

Marster was good to slaves. Don't believe in just lashing 'em. He'd not be brutal, but he'd kill 'em dead right on the spot. Ova-seers'd git after 'em and whop 'em down.

We had to steal away at night to have church on de ditch bank, and crawl home on de belly. Once overseers heard us prayin', give us each one hundred lashes.

Freedom was declared, but de slaves didn't know it. We'se refugees, young mistress and masta brought us out to keep us fron being free. Dey toll us de Yankees would kill us iffen dey found us. We was a dodgin' in and out, runnin' from de Yankees. We was free and didn't know it. Ah lost mah baby; it's buried some where on de road.

Dey turn us loose in the world. Not a penny. Oh, dey was awful times. We just woked about from place to place after freedom. Hiahd to white people by month, week, day.[4]

As Elvira Boles suggests, emancipation brought economic difficulties of its own. Most slaves thought freedom would mean more than self-ownership; they expected a measure of economic security and independence that only landownership could bring them. But the government pledge of "forty acres and a mule" became a dream deferred. As Isaac Crawford, born a slave in Holmes County, recalled: "I didn't know bout freedom and I didn't care bout it. They didn't give no land nor no mules away as I ever know'd of."[5] Impoverished and illiterate, emancipated slaves faced a labor market that did not guarantee them the one "right" they had under slavery—the right to subsistence.[6] Working as sharecroppers and wage laborers was better than slaving; but to those at the bottom, Holmes County's post-emancipation economic order must have looked depressingly familiar.

Although Reconstruction failed to alter fundamentally the plantation economy, it was a rousing period of black political and social mobilization. In Holmes County, African Americans were elected to a number of offices: sheriff, state senator and representative, county supervisor, tax assessor, circuit clerk, and coroner. The majority of posts were filled by their white Republican allies, mostly northern "carpetbaggers." Local political authority and control of the judiciary translated into increased government services and favorable public policies for blacks. With the help of the Freedmen's Bureau, R. A. Simmons, a Dartmouth graduate of mixed race, helped set up the county's first schools for blacks. After taking over the Richland School for black use, Simmons marched his students through town in a show of racial pride and strength.[7]

White resistance to Radical Reconstruction in Holmes County was openly terrorist. Young zealots joined Heggie's Scouts, and the Red Shirts attracted a widespread membership, including some of the county's most respected white citizens. Despite the presence of federal troops, both white supremacist groups shunned the Klan's tactics of secrecy. "The secret order of the Ku Klux Klan," a county newspaper later recalled, "terrorized the evil doers by night and the bolder Red Shirts kept their colors flying by day."[8] According to an admiring historian, Heggie's Scouts "did not disguise themselves, operated in open daylight, and their object was to make negroes humble by visiting terrible punishment upon them. . . . They often whipped negroes who refused to work. . . . Sometimes when the blacks were especially troublesome the 'Scouts' had orders to kill every one they met."[9] Organized by the Democratic Party, the Red Shirts likewise used violence and intimidation to stem the tide of black political and social power; but the group's tactically astute leaders sponsored social activities to keep its agenda at the center of white social and cultural life. Red Shirt parades, picnics, parties, and balls were "the greatest social gatherings possible . . . and kept alive the enthusiasm [for the restoration of the old political and social order]."[10]

With Northern support waning and Mississippi whites committed to seizing power at any cost, the ruling Republican coalition of blacks, carpetbaggers, and a few native "scalawags" was in trouble as the 1875 election approached. African Americans in Holmes County, as in the rest of the state, were the junior partners of this coalition. In August 1875, Wiley Hill, Holmes County's black tax assessor, challenged white political domination within the Republican Party by publicly criticizing and insulting J. G. Mills, a leading white Republican. A few days later, Hill and a black bystander were killed by Mills and another prominent white Republican in a shootout inside the courthouse. Many witnesses maintained that Hill had been unarmed.[11] Transplanted northerners, themselves often the targets of terrorist attacks, did a great deal for black Holmes Countians during Reconstruction. Nevertheless, this incident shows that southerners were not the only whites intent on keeping blacks in their "place"—and through violence if necessary.

But even if the Republican Party in Holmes County had been united, it would have made little difference in the election of 1875. Armed whites repulsed blacks from the polls. In one Holmes County community, Democrats went so far as to mount a cannon at the polling place.[12] At another, election officials drew a line in front of the ballot box and dared any black to cross.[13] Thus Reconstruction—that radical experiment in interracial democracy—came to an end, and conservative white rule was restored.

Already disenfranchised by violence and fraud, all but a small fraction of Holmes County blacks were formally excluded from the voting booth by the literacy, residency, and poll-tax requirements of the 1890 state constitution. Between 1890 and 1964, only twenty-six African Americans were allowed to register to vote in Holmes County.[14] Following Reconstruction, a few black Holmes Countians remained active in the moribund Republican Party, which ran neither local nor state candidates. They kept alive a flicker of black political activism by voting in presidential elections and participating in state party conventions, but their practical political effect was nil. Within ten years of emancipation, the U.S. Constitution's Fifteenth Amendment notwithstanding, almost all black Holmes Countians were denied the ballot.

African-American life in Holmes County between Reconstruction and the Civil Rights Movement—the Second Reconstruction—was bleak. Most blacks labored as tenants on white plantations and farms. In 1925, more than 90 percent of all farmers in Holmes County were tenants, and 94 percent of the people on tenant farms were black.[15] Theoretically, sharecropping afforded blacks more control over their time, work, and household arrangements than did wage labor.[16] In practice, however, sharecroppers existed in a state of virtual peonage, bound to the land, their debts, and their landlords. Most black Holmes Countians remember sharecropping as economic bondage. Reflecting back on forty years as a sharecropper, Mrs. Catherine Jefferson commented to her *Bloodlines* interviewers that "[i]t seems like I just been a slave all the way from down then til now."[17]

The ruling planter class in Holmes County was determined to maintain a dependent plantation labor force, and education for blacks suffered as a result. As Neil R. McMillen contends in *Dark Journey: Black Mississippians in the Age of Jim Crow,* "Throughout the Jim Crow era, the single greatest impediment to better Afro-American schools was white fear of the revolutionary social and economic implications of educating a subservient workforce."[18] When the federal government offered to build a modern, multiroom vocational school in 1939, the Holmes County Board of Education voted to table the issue in order to determine "whether white neighboring planters would approve of it."[19] The school was eventually built; but, like all others in Holmes County, it was structured to produce efficient, disciplined, and docile laborers.

Schools set up by the Freedmen's Bureau continued to operate into the twentieth century, but the vast majority of blacks were educated in one-room grammar schools situated in or adjacent to churches and staffed by teachers whose own schooling was unlikely to have exceeded the ninth grade.[20] In 1937, ninety-four black schools were scattered around the county, including many built with the help of northern philanthropic money, especially the Rosenwald Fund.[21] Since Rosenwald grants required matching local support, black Holmes Countians often had to dig into their own pockets. Public support for the schools was minimal. According to school district records for Holmes County in the 1938–1939 school year, an average of $33.22 was spent on instruction for each white student, compared to $2.63 spent on each black.[22] Many black children's families could not afford to lose a hand in the field; nor could they pay for books or school clothes.[23] Those who were able went to school for four months out of the year until 1940, when the academic year was extended to six months. Split sessions that required school attendance during the hottest summer months continued into the 1960s, thus ensuring that white planters had an adequate supply of cheap labor to harvest their cotton in the fall. As the interviews with Leola Blackmon and William Eskridge make plain, local blacks—in contrast to civil rights lawyers—often regarded split sessions as a more pressing problem than school segregation. Although the state legislature had long since provided for the transportation of white children to school, black children walked until 1950, when Holmes County's first bus route for black students was established. And until that year, only four black public schools in the county offered instruction through the ninth grade.[24]

Schooling was but one piece in a complex pattern of racial segregation designed to maintain white control. In Mississippi, white supremacy was reasserted after Reconstruction with such vigor that Jim Crow custom often proceeded without the backing of Jim Crow law.[25] Reinforced by the pervasive threat of violence against nonconformists, the social code in Holmes County required blacks to feign deference in all things. African Americans got down off the raised sidewalk when whites approached. They went to the back door of snack bars, train depots, and white homes. Black men averted their eyes when white women passed. "Now I don't care how many white peoples was in [the store]," Richard West told a high school interviewer, "you waited til they got waited on. If they kept comin' in, you kept waiting."[26] Another black Holmes Countian reported in 1940 that it was illegal for black drivers to pass cars driven by whites, "because the black man might stir up dust that would get on the white folks."[27] In Holmes County, the "place" of blacks was so severely circumscribed that any act that could be construed as uppity was dangerous. "I can remember," related Mrs. Catherine Jefferson in *Bloodlines*, "you wasn't allowed to wear white shirts in town. If you did, the white people would whoop ya. Also couldn't buy a coca cola. . . . They say niggers didn't have no reason with no coca cola, and it was costing five cents at the time."[28]

Racial etiquette was enforced by racial violence. Between 1889 and 1945, there were eight reported lynchings in Holmes County;[29] but even a cursory investigation turns up many more. According to Richard West, suspected murderer Sloan Allen was forced to dig his own grave and to build the fire over which he was boiled alive. That lynching occurred in 1893.[30] In 1923, a black boy from Holmes County borrowed fifty cents from a white landowner. The boy repaid the loan a few days later but refused to pay ten cents for interest. Later that evening, when a mob was unable to find the boy, they shot and killed an eighteen-year-old black girl instead.[31] In 1946, five Holmes County whites admitted that they brutally beat (but denied killing) a black tenant farmer who was accused of stealing a saddle. The man was found two days later floating in a bayou; his two stepsons confessed to having taken the saddle. The five landowners—the only suspected lynchers brought to trial in Holmes County history—were found not guilty of manslaughter. The all-white jury deliberated for four minutes.[32]

Lynching was the most brutal means of instilling fear in the black populace and of maintaining social control. Whites justified lynching as a deterrent against the rape of white women by black men, but most blacks in Holmes County were lynched ostensibly because they were suspected of murder. Still, the burning passion aroused by the thought of a black man with a white woman cost at least one Holmes Countian his life. When Booker T. Burch's love affair with a white woman was discovered in 1936, reports a student essay, he was mercilessly tortured, castrated, weighted with heavy chains, and drowned in a pond.[33]

Of course, intimacy between white men and black women in Holmes County dates back to slavery. Whether exploitative, commercial, or based on mutual affection, these relationships raised both black and white eyebrows but were nevertheless common. As one elderly Holmes Countian recalls, "Some white women had the police come from Jackson, go up there and raid the City Hotel, and black women come flying out of there! See, the children they was having were the ones gonna be the trouble. The white people called 'em 'half-white niggers.' "[34] The "mongrelization of the race" was the white supremacist's nightmare, but that did not keep white men from sleeping with black women. As Neil McMillen writes, "The appetites of the flesh were not easily governed by the logic of Jim Crow and the color line was rarely so permeable as when it passed through the bedroom."[35]

Black resistance to Jim Crow subjugation bubbled just beneath the surface of public life. Individual whites and blacks could form lasting friendships, but these were cast in the mold of white paternalism. Racial interaction was usually a charade. A mask of deference and contentment was put on for white folk, hiding the depths of black alienation. In search of economic opportunity and human dignity, thousands of black Holmes Countians simply left for northern cities between 1910 and

1950. Discontent was especially pointed for veterans of military service. Returning to Holmes County from world wars in which they were called to sacrifice their lives in the name of democracy, black soldiers expected social conditions to change. "I figure that if I can go int' Uncle Sam's army to try an' fight for America," states Cooper Howard in his interview, "I can come back and be counted as an American. Not as somebody that's throwed aside." Some black veterans used their paychecks to purchase land of their own, thereby insulating themselves from white control, and many later figured prominently in the struggle for racial justice.

Black landownership was the critical resource in the development of a strong Holmes County Movement. Although the vast majority of black Holmes Countians worked as tenants, a higher proportion of land has been owned by African Americans in Holmes County than in most of the state's other counties. Until 1940, much of this land was located in the hillier sections of the county, on tracts that whites could not afford to cultivate—relatively inaccessible land prone to erosion and soil depletion. Most black-owned farms barely managed to stay solvent, but those farmers who raised hogs, cows, chickens, and vegetables on land of their own exercised a degree of self-direction unheard of on the plantation.

In 1940, the New Deal's Farm Security Administration (FSA) purchased five failing plantations in the Delta community of Mileston and sold the 9,580 acres of fertile land to 107 sharecropping families on long-term, low-interest mortgages. At first, 36 of the units were owned and farmed collectively, but under congressional pressure the FSA reorganized them into individually owned family farms. Each of these farms typically included 60 acres of land, a screened home, a smokehouse, and a barn. Farmers also received mules, seed, tools, canning jars, and other supplies. One of 30 such model communities nationwide, Mileston boasted a cooperative store and cotton gin, a repair shop, and a modern school. The FSA also provided medical care and technical assistance to families for the development of detailed farm and home plans. Assaulted by Congress for its socialist bent, the FSA was eventually disbanded; but in Holmes County the seeds for social change had been planted.[36]

At first, it seems, white planters did not take seriously this radical challenge to their agrarian order. Convinced that black sharecroppers could not successfully manage their own farms, one planter, while signing his land over to the FSA, boasted to the assembled blacks that he would have his land back in ten years. Still in her home fifty years later, Mrs. Mary Hayes chuckled as she recalled that comment. With mechanized agriculture and other trends undermining the small family farm, the Mileston farmers never had incomes much above subsistence; but what they did have was more threatening to the caste system: independence, pride, and control of their destiny. Mrs. Hayes is the widow of Ralthus Hayes, a crucial leader in the county's civil rights struggle. During a videotaped interview with a high school student, she characterized their land as "a gift from the Lord. . . . Had your own stuff then, wadn't dependent on the white man for nothing. If you didn't make it, that was your fault."[37]

Emancipation from slavery was incomplete because blacks did not receive land, but in 1940 the federal government salvaged the dream of "forty acres and a mule" for some black Holmes Countians. By addressing the underlying causes of persistent rural poverty, the Mileston Farm Project created an independent landed class out of a depressed rural tenantry.[38] In this way, it gave Holmes County blacks a beachhead of economic security from which to fight for a more successful Second Reconstruction.

The Second Reconstruction was inaugurated by the 1954 *Brown v. Board of Education* ruling that finally found the racial segregation of public schools unconstitutional. Southern whites resisted the Supreme Court decision with a fervor that reached hysterical proportions in Mississippi. The magnolia state gave birth to the Citizens' Council, the preeminent organizational vehicle of rabid southern resistance to desegregation. Holmes County's chapter of this "country club Klan" was the second formed in the nation.[39] Led by the most "respectable" whites, it employed tactics more sophisticated than those used by the Klan. The Citizens' Council specialized in propaganda, lobbying, and economic reprisal—intimidating blacks who challenged the caste system by firing them from their jobs, refusing them credit, denying them loans, and putting them off farms. The Council successfully enforced a rigid racial orthodoxy among Mississippi whites and dominated local, county, and state politics from 1954 to 1964. Gubernatorial candidates outdid each other trying to convince voters of their uncompromising commitment to white supremacy. And the Mississippi legislature enacted a creative array of statutes to safeguard the sociopolitical subjugation of its black constitutents.[40] The Citizens' Council prided itself on its aversion to Klan tactics, but its extremist rhetoric encouraged violence against blacks.

Race relations in Holmes County were highly charged even before the *Brown* decision. In January 1954, a young black Holmes Countian named Eddie Noel shot and killed a white storeowner during an argument. After two shootouts and a massive manhunt, two more Holmes County whites lay dead and another two were seriously injured by bullets from Noel's .22 bolt-action rifle. To whites this was cold-blooded murder. To blacks it represented a courageous personal stance born of pent-up bitterness. Eddie Noel eventually turned himself in, but he remains a folk hero in the black community to this day. He was no revolutionary, but the episode reminded whites and blacks alike what form black resistance to white domination could take.

The *Brown* decision and the Eddie Noel incident sharpened the siege mentality of Holmes County whites. When one of their own—newspaper publisher Hazel Brannon Smith—condemned in print the July 1954 shooting of a black man as he obeyed the sheriff's order to "get goin'," she was branded a traitor and lost many of her friends overnight. A segregationist, Smith nevertheless actively opposed the Citizens' Council. White reaction to her courageous stance (libel suits, advertisers' boycotts, a rival newspaper started by Citizens' Council activists, and social ostracism) pushed Smith further and further into a no-man's land between the races. By the early 1960s, she had become a valuable ally of the Civil Rights Movement, but her domineering paternalism alienated many black activists. In a charged field of racial polarization, Hazel Brannon Smith exemplified the valiance, trials, and limitations of white liberals.

African Americans, of course, were the real victims of organized racism. Black farmers struggled to hold onto their land in the face of determined white attempts to break black landowners by squeezing their credit. Bodies were found in lakes as violence against blacks mounted.[41] In May 1955, Reverend George Lee was shot while driving his car and died in the crash. Lee had been organizing a voter registration campaign in Humphreys County, adjacent to Holmes County. In August 1955, Emmett Till was murdered for speaking offhandedly to a white woman in neighboring Leflore County. The fourteen-year-old's lynching received worldwide attention and helped spark the Civil Rights Movement.

The Citizens' Council in Holmes County flexed its muscles in September 1955 by organizing a mass meeting of more than five hundred citizens to drive two white families from the county. Their crime? Practicing social equality on Providence Farm, a biracial community with a doctor's clinic, credit union, and cooperative store. A forerunner of the Civil Rights Movement, Providence Farm was established in the 1930s by northern Christian Socialists as an experiment in cooperative agriculture. The communal farming failed, but the wrath of the Citizens' Council suggests Providence's potency as a witness to social and racial justice. "It was like when the Yankees came through," related a black leader on the farm to a student interviewer. "They was tired of people living in slavery, was trying to let you come out on your own. . . . They wanted everybody to have equal."[42] If it looked forward to the civil rights struggle, Providence Farm also looked back to emancipation and Reconstruction.

The Holmes County Movement

Like blacks across the nation, Holmes Countians followed the national Civil Rights Movement as it was born in Montgomery, as it gathered momentum from the student sit-ins, and as it hit Mississippi with the freedom rides. In the summer of 1962, as national attention began to focus on James Meredith's attempt to integrate Ole Miss, the Movement reached neighboring Leflore County as a small cadre of young black workers with the Student Nonviolent Coordinating Committee (SNCC) began trying to register black voters. Leflore County officials responded to SNCC's organizing activities by cutting off federal food commodities to the county's 22,000 poorest citizens, siccing dogs on peaceful marchers, and arresting leaders. Unofficial resistance was even sharper. Local whites ransacked the SNCC office and eventually succeeded in burning it down. SNCC workers and local sympathizers were beaten and shot. One white resident explained to *New York Times* reporter Claude Sitton, "We killed two-month-old Indian babies to take this country, and now they want us to give it away to the niggers."[43]

Despite the dangers, a small group of Mileston farmers journeyed to Greenwood in the early spring of 1963 and asked SNCC workers to bring the Movement to Holmes County. Having spent upwards of six months trying to stir Greenwood's black community out of its quiescence, SNCC immediately sent an organizer to Mileston. John Ball taught the Mileston farmers about voter registration—about the form with twenty-one questions; about the requirement that they be able to read, write, and interpret any of the 285 sections of the state constitution to the satisfaction of the registrar; about the new law allowing voters to object to the moral character of new registrants; and about the other recent law requiring that the names of voter applicants be published in local newspapers. Undaunted, between fourteen and twenty-one blacks, almost all Mileston landowners, attempted to register to vote on April 9, 1963.

Retribution was swift. The home of Hartman Turnbow, the first black to step forward when the group was confronted by the sheriff on the courthouse lawn, was firebombed and riddled with bullets. Turnbow fired back with his automatic rifle. The next morning, the sheriff arrested Turnbow for arson, along with Bob Moses and three other SNCC workers. This move prompted the U.S. Department of Justice to intervene with a federal suit seeking an injunction against Sheriff Smith for intimidating black citizens from registering to vote. This first incident set the pattern for the Holmes County Movement: guidance from outside civil rights workers, bold action by local blacks, often violent white reprisal, armed black self-defense, repression by local officials, and legal redress reluctantly undertaken by the Justice Department.

As Holmes County blacks took their first unflinching steps toward freedom and bore the consequences in the spring of 1963, national attention was riveted on Birmingham, Alabama, where Martin Luther King's Southern Christian Leadership Conference was locked in battle with Bull Connor's forces. Each campaign represents a different tradition within the Civil Rights Movement. As Bob Moses argues, Birmingham typifies the community *mobilizing* tradition as large numbers of people, often spurred by King's oratory, were mobilized in pursuit of a specific goal—the desegregation of public facilities. Though rooted in local commitment, this strategy depended on widespread media coverage, large-scale events, and outside leadership. The Holmes County Movement, by contrast, epitomizes the community *organizing* tradition developed by SNCC in Mississippi. Organizers immersed themselves in communities outside the nation's public eye and sought to politicize residents around everyday problems and issues. Inspired by Ella Baker and exemplified by Bob Moses, the community organizing tradition sought to develop indigenous leadership and to build an organizational vehicle owned by local people that would carry their agenda over the long haul.[44]

That organizational vehicle was the Mississippi Freedom Democratic Party. Nowhere did it develop into a stronger political entity than in Holmes County, where it brought the election in 1967 of the first black to the Mississippi legislature since Reconstruction, and where it survives to this day. Trying to exercise the vote consumed the Movement's energies through the summer of 1965, when school integration became yet another major organizing focus. The detailed chronology of events at the back of this book provides a narrative skeleton of the Holmes County and national Movements.

Progress for the Civil Rights Movement was torturous everywhere, but Holmes County activists faced a particularly steep uphill climb owing to the county's rural character. The proximity of urban blacks in densely populated neighborhoods encouraged the development of independent institutions and a strong sense of community,[45] whereas black Holmes Countians were scattered around the countryside in isolated pockets. To be sure, a sense of community developed in rural areas, too, and was reinforced at church, family gatherings, fish fries, barbecues, juke houses, and the Saturday sojourn into town; but the lives of rural blacks were more severely circumscribed than those of urban blacks. "Only public was white people," explains a black Holmes Countian. "There wasn't no black public, 'cause they didn't get together for nothing but to go to church and go to the fields."[46] Blacks living in cities could also develop a group identity around their shared position in the workplace, where white domination was less personal and more distant than in households and on rural farms.[47] As many of the interviews in this volume attest, whites were so intent on maintaining social control in rural areas that when blacks did meet, an informer was often present to bring word back to his white master.

The biggest obstacle to the Holmes County Movement was the character of the rural church. The black church functioned as the crucial resource of the national Civil Rights Movement, providing it with leadership, an organized following, a financial base, communications networks, institutionalized charisma, meeting places, and an ideological framework.[48] In Holmes County, however, the black church was a belated, reluctant convert to the Movement. Almost all of the county's one hundred small black churches were pastored by part-time ministers whose full-time livelihoods made them as economically dependent on the white elite as anybody else. Many of these churches held full services only on alternate Sundays or once a month; others were located on plantations, where they could be monitored by planters who sometimes contributed to church coffers. The strongest independent black institution of all, these churches nevertheless developed in a field of white domination.

Movement activists worked through church networks because the church was the center of black community life. As an institution, however, the black church provided little more than space for citizenship classes, freedom schools, and community meetings. And when churches did align themselves with the Movement, it was usually because the deacons overruled the pastors. Of course, religion infused the Movement from the outset. Prayer, religious oratory, and biblical themes set the tone of Movement gatherings, and participants saw themselves as part of the timeless struggle between good and evil. Church songs were changed to make explicit the connection between theology and activism. "Woke up this morning with my mind stayed on Jesus," for instance, was altered to provide the title of this book, and "God is on our side" is a favorite verse from "We Shall Overcome." Activists felt assured of eventual victory because on their side were Moses, the Old Testament prophets, Jesus of Nazareth, and God Almighty.

If the black church was the crucial resource for the national Civil Rights Movement, black landownership filled that role for the Holmes County Movement. Independent landowners, who were often poor "dirt farmers," formed the backbone of the Holmes County Movement. As the two interviews with Carroll Countians suggest, civil rights activism in most other Mississippi counties lacked the strength and vitality of the Holmes County Movement, primarily because other local Movements were not buttressed by black landowners. Black insurgency in Holmes County was rooted in the economic independence provided by landownership. Without that base, local Movements could be overwhelmed by the many arms of white power. All across the rural South, black-owned land was an absolutely essential resource for the Civil Rights Movement.

Holmes County diverges from the accepted picture of the Civil Rights Movement in other important ways as well—not because Holmes County is exceptional, but because the accepted picture of the Movement has been unduly colored by attention to national leaders and a few urban Movement centers. The interviews that follow suggest that in the countryside, out of the glare of television lights, armed self-defense was preached, practiced, and effective. Women played crucial roles. Organizational bickering between the Southern Christian Leadership Conference (SCLC), the Congress of Racial Equality (CORE), the NAACP, and SNCC was less pronounced at the local level. Yet fissures along the lines of social class divided local ranks. Movement finances were often raised locally. Head Start reflected Movement values until the local white elite and the federal government perceived the danger of institutionalizing black empowerment. Partially co-opted, Head Start and other antipoverty programs siphoned local leadership from the Movement. Thus, the oral histories that follow, free of leveling interpretation and bias, provide abundant fodder for analysis by historians, sociologists, and activists.

Minds Stayed on Freedom confirms that external leaders, organizers, volunteers, lawyers, national networks, and philanthropy were important to the struggle for racial justice in the South. The national Movement's two great speakers—Martin Luther King, Jr., and Fannie Lou Hamer— energized Holmes Countians wherever they were heard. And without the SNCC organizers, the Movement in Holmes County may never have gotten off the ground. Volunteers, especially a husband-and-wife team whose presence from 1964 to 1969 made the local Movement unique, provided essential support. Lawyers' groups were also important; in Holmes County alone, 124 Movement-related lawsuits were filed. National Movement networks, especially the citizenship workshops sponsored by SCLC and the Highlander Folk School, trained activists who passed on their skills at the local level. Finally, outside benefactors helped sustain the Holmes County Movement.

These people were all important, but they were supporting actors. *Minds Stayed on Freedom* reminds us that ordinary black folk were often the real heroes. Still unsung, these home-grown activists finally have an opportunity to tell their stories in the interviews that follow.

Holmes County Today

The Civil Rights Movement has transformed Holmes County. Today, Mississippi boasts the largest number of black elected officials in the nation, and Holmes County has the largest bloc of any county in the state. Public facilities are no longer segregated by law. Police violence has been substantially curbed. Job opportunities have widened far beyond domestic service and plantation labor. In short, personal and political freedom is now largely a reality for black Holmes Countians.

But Jim Crow is not dead. Although the last "white" and "colored" signs came down from doctors' waiting rooms (in 1979!), churches are still segregated. Schools remain segregated as well, because whites set up private academies to skirt *Brown v. Board of Education.* Holmes County whites have "advanced" to the point where they publicly defend these academies on the grounds that the instruction there is better than in the public schools; but during the fall of 1989, East Holmes Academy refused to play a football game because the opposition's team included a black running back.

Like their urban counterparts in the North and South, black youths in Holmes County are still dealt a hand that makes a mockery of the United States as the land of opportunity. With fearful regularity, college graduates in Holmes County end up bagging groceries, driving tractors, and ginning cotton for minimum wage. Hundreds of black Holmes Countians commute upwards of fifty miles each day to labor at low-paying, high-risk jobs in chicken and catfish processing plants. A drastic rate of black land loss also points up the economic insecurity of blacks. In 1979, black per capita income was $2,292—38 percent of the white figure.[49] Prior to 1960, Holmes County ranked as one of the nation's poorest counties. Today, despite the preponderance of black elected officials, the county retains that dubious distinction. The Civil Rights Movement has failed to yield substantial economic improvement for Holmes County blacks, a failure that is mirrored nationwide.

Perhaps the saga of Eddie Carthan best illustrates the achievements and limitations of the Civil Rights Movement. As the fourteen-year-old son of a Mileston farmer, Carthan was arrested at a civil rights demonstration with his grandfather. He took to heart the lessons he had been taught in the Movement's "freedom schools," resolving to get the best education possible in order to serve his people. He received a master's degree in business administration, worked for the U.S. Commerce Department, and began his own business. By small-town standards, Carthan was already a successful businessman by the time he celebrated his twenty-fifth birthday. He then served as president of the Holmes County Board of Education. Elected in 1977 as the first black mayor of a biracial Delta town since Reconstruction, Carthan symbolized the breakthroughs of the Civil Rights Movement.

But Mayor Carthan was not content merely holding a political *position;* he insisted on exercising political *power* in the interests of his constituency.

By aggressively pursuing federal funds, he managed to rack up an impressive list of accomplishments: a housing weatherization and rehabilitation program, a daycare center, a feeding program for the elderly, twenty-four-hour police service, paved roads in the black sections of town, a low-income housing development, and eighty new jobs. Their economic interests threatened by the resultant black independence, Delta planters and Tchula businessmen engineered Carthan's political downfall. They made an example out of Eddie Carthan in a series of frame-ups that discredited the mayor and warned against aggressive, progressive black leadership. "It threatens a whole system of justice," explained former U.S. Attorney General Ramsay Clark. "Its racial implications are overwhelming. It's so clearly part of an effort to destroy young black talent." Guilty, at worst, of managerial oversights, Carthan was put on trial for capital murder. Amnesty International monitored the trial. Carthan was acquitted but spent more than a year in jail for other alleged offenses.[50] The message from the white elite was unmistakable: You can hold political office, but attempts to wield political power in a manner that challenges our economic dominance will not be tolerated.

If the first Reconstruction ultimately signified "the resiliency of an old ruling class rather than the triumph of a new order,"[51] the Civil Rights Movement is threatened by the same fate. Our task is to keep chipping away at injustice and, in so doing, to further these unfinished revolutions. By recounting history from the bottom up, this book shows how ordinary people can generate power to shape their own destiny. The Rural Organizing and Cultural Center makes the following interviews available in the hope that they will inspire people, wherever they might be, to take up hammer and chisel and start chipping.

NOTES

The author would like to thank Arnett Lewis, Ann Brown, and Leroy Johnson of the Rural Organizing and Cultural Center for their careful scrutiny of the manuscript and their insightful comments. I am also grateful to Neil McMillen, Aldon Morris, Judith Porter, and David Karen for their helpful reviews. Thanks also to Sue Sojourner for taking time off from her own work on the Holmes County Movement to help in the preparation of this book. I would like to acknowledge with deep appreciation the help and encouragement of Sal Asher. Finally, I want to thank the *Minds* authors. They've been extraordinary colleagues.

1. Howard Zinn, *A People's History on the United States* (New York: Harper and Row, 1980), p. 570.

2. Alexander Cockburn, "Beat the Devil," *The Nation*, June 18, 1990, p. 846.

3. Holmes County Works Progress Administration (WPA) Files, Supplementary to Assignment No. 14, "Outlaw Days," Mississippi Department of Archives and History.

4. George P. Rawick, ed., *The American Slave: A Composite Autobiography,* Vol. 2 of *Texas Narratives,* Part 1 (West Point, Conn.: Greenwood Press, 1979), pp. 336–339.

5. George P. Rawick, ed., *The American Slave: A Composite Autobiography,* Vol. 8 of *Arkansas Narratives* (West Point, Conn.: Greenwood Press, 1972), p. 58.

6. Eric Foner, *Nothing But Freedom: Emancipation and Its Legacy* (Baton Rouge: Louisiana State University Press, 1983), p. 57.

7. Holmes County WPA Files, "History of Holmes County: Reconstruction," Mississippi Department of Archives and History.

8. Jack Brumby, "Holmes County—Today and Yesterday," *Lexington Advertiser* (100th Anniversary Edition, 1937), p. 6.

9. Fred M. Witty, "Reconstruction in Carroll and Montgomery Counties," *Publications of the Mississippi Historical Society,* Vol. 10 (1909), pp. 129–130.

10. Brumby, "Holmes County."

11. *Weekly Jackson Pilot,* issues from August 7 through September 11, 1875.

12. Holmes County WPA Files, "History of Holmes County: Reconstruction."

13. Holmes County WPA Files, Assignment No. 14, "Interview with Mr. Wirt Smith, 8/18/36," Mississippi Department of Archives and History.

14. John Hersey, "A Life for a Vote," *Saturday Evening Post,* September 26, 1964, p. 34.

15. James W. Loewen and Charles Sallis, eds., *Mississippi: Conflict and Change* (New York: Pantheon, 1980), p. 207; United States Department of Commerce, *Census of Agriculture: 1925–Mississippi,* County Table V ("Farm Population by Age, Sex, Color, and Tenure: 1925"), p. 888.

16. Foner, *Nothing But Freedom,* p. 55.

17. John Darjean, "Mrs. Catherine Jefferson: 'Seems Like I Just Been a Slave,' " *Bloodlines,* Vol. 1 (Summer 1988), p. 38.

18. Neil R. McMillen, *Dark Journey: Black Mississippians in the Age of Jim Crow* (Urbana and Chicago: University of Illinois Press, 1989), p. 90.

19. Holmes County School System, "Official Minutes of the Board of Education, 1931–1932." Quoted in Sylvia Reedy Gist, "Educational Arrangements for Blacks in Holmes County, Mississippi, Prior to 1950," an unpublished paper (1989), p. 13.

20. Gist, "Educational Arrangements," p. 10.

21. Holmes County WPA Files, "Negro Education," Mississippi Department of Archives and History.

22. Holmes County WPA Files, "Holmes County School Census and Statistics for Session 1938–1939," Mississippi Department of Archives and History.

23. McMillen, *Dark Journey,* p. 25.

24. Gist, "Educational Arrangements," pp. 15–17.

25. McMillen, *Dark Journey,* p. 10.

26. Videotaped interview with Richard West, by Sally Common (April 1990).

27. Quoted in McMillen, *Dark Journey,* p. 11.

28. Darjean, "Mrs. Catherine Jefferson," p. 33.

29. McMillen, *Dark Journey,* p. 231.

30. Richard West interview; "Lynchings" Vertical File, Mississippi Department of Archives and History.

31. "Lynchings" Vertical File; "Negro Girl Shot Down by a Mob at Pickens," *Memphis Commercial Appeal,* October 7, 1923.

32. "Six White Land-Owners Charged With Murder in Flogging Upstate," *Jackson Daily News,* July 30, 1946; "Stepsons of Lynch Victim Admit Theft for Which He Was Whipped," *Jackson Clarion Ledger,* August 1, 1946; "Five Men Freed on Manslaughter in Negro's Death," *Lexington Advertiser,* October 24, 1946, p. 1.

33. Sheri Reed, "Black-Owned Land and Life on the Plantation," an unpublished paper (1986).

34. Richard West interview.

35. McMillen, *Dark Journey*, p. 14.

36. James D. Holley, "The New Deal and Farm Tenancy: Rural Resettlement in Arkansas, Louisiana, and Mississippi," Ph.D. dissertation, Louisiana State University (1969); Lester M. Salamon, "The Time Dimension in Policy Evaluation: The Case of the New Deal Land Reform Experiments," an unpublished paper (1975); videotaped interview with Mary Hayes, by Rhonda Washington (April 1990).

37. Mary Hayes interview.

38. Salamon, "The Time Dimension," p. 39.

39. William Lee Miller, "People in Mississippi: Trial by Tape Recorder," *Reporter,* No. 13 (December 15, 1955), p. 28.

40. See Neil R. McMillen, *The Citizens' Council: Organized Resistance to the Second Reconstruction, 1954-64* (Urbana: University of Illinois Press, 1971).

41. Hersey, "A Life for a Vote," p. 37.

42. Videotaped interview with Fannye Booker, by Janice Brand (May 1990); Miller, "People in Mississippi," pp. 27–30.

43. Claude Sitton, "Tension Builds Up After Gun Attack: Voter Registration Drive Is Intensified After Leader Is Wounded by Volley," *New York Times,* April 6, 1963, p. 20.

44. Robert P. Moses et al., "The Algebra Project: Organizing in the Spirit of Ella," *Harvard Educational Review,* Vol. 59 (November 1989), pp. 424–428.

45. Aldon D. Morris, *The Origins of the Civil Rights Movement* (New York: Free Press, 1984), p. 79.

46. Richard West interview.

47. Morris, *The Origins of the Civil Rights Movement,* pp. 78–79.

48. Ibid., pp. 4–12, 77.

49. United States Department of Commerce, *1980 Census of Population: Number of Inhabitants, Mississippi,* Vol. 1, Part 26, Table 186 ("Labor Force Status in 1979 and Income Characteristics in 1979 by Race and Spanish Origin by Counties: 1980") (Washington, D.C.: GPO, 1983), p. 26-413.

50. John Kincaid, "Beyond the Voting Rights Act: White Responses to Black Political Power in Tchula, Mississippi," *The Journal of Federalism,* Vol. 16 (Fall 1986), pp. 155–172; Sheila Collins, "Crucifixion in Mississippi," *Caribbean Times* (London), June 10, 1983; NBC Sunday Today, "Eddie Carthan: Fallen Star," November 20, 1988.

51. Foner, *Nothing But Freedom,* p. 72.

REV. J. J. RUSSELL &
MRS. ERMA RUSSELL

*Holmes County's Dr. and Mrs.
Martin Luther King, Jr.*

KENNETH SALLIS, WILLA WILLIAMS,
& JENNIFER DIXON

Reverend and Mrs. Russell are an elderly couple who reside in the Mileston community south of Tchula. They were two of the first participants in the Holmes County Movement. In the spring of 1963, when others were too scared to even come to a meeting, the Russells held meetings in their home with other Mileston farmers like the Carnegies, the Mitchells, the Howards, and the Turnbows. Reverend Russell was one of the first fourteen blacks who went to the courthouse to try to register to vote on April 9, 1963.

Reverend Russell is a religious man dedicated to the gospel and the church. He was the only preacher with the conviction and the courage to lead the Movement, but he paid a great price for it. One of his churches was burned, and the windows were knocked out of another. Then people refused to let him preach in their churches for fear that their church buildings would be vandalized. So Reverend Russell preached in his own home until other communities opened up to the Movement.

Mrs. Russell has stood beside her husband throughout their life together. She had to stay at home a lot with their children, but she was secretary of the health clinic and actively supported the Movement.

We did this interview in class in front of the other students so we could all learn from it. Reverend Russell is a firm believer in nonviolence. He says it's a sword that cuts without wounding. All the students in our class, and even the teacher, got excited and craned their necks forward to see the pistol when Reverend Russell said he was going to pull out his weapon. He reached into his case and brought out his Bible instead!

[In the following interview, the speakers are Reverend J. J. Russell (**RR**) and Mrs. Erma Russell (**MR**).]

Mr. J. J. Russell and Mrs. Russell, how did the Civil Rights Movement begin for y'all in Holmes County?

RR: The Civil Rights Movement began in Holmes County in the Mileston community. When we was first started, we met and we held classes. We had classes goin' on in every community which teach you how to fill out those forms [to register to vote].

Some people couldn't read and write, but we taught them how to read and write and to fill out those blanks. We had a form we s'posed to fill out with twenty-one questions before you could pass the test. Also, you had to interp'et 'bout two hundred eighty-five sections of the Constitution of Mississippi, which didn't many people know about. And so we had to study those laws and learn how to interp'et questions so you could pass it. You gotta go to the courthouse and the circuit clerk.

Twenty-one of us went to the courthouse and asked could we register to vote. The high sheriff, deputies, and many other plain-clothed policemen was on duty. They challenged us. We told them we wanted to redishter [register]. They said, "For what?"

We said, "To vote," and they was soundin' off, talking and hollerin'. But we didn't get excited because we had men from Justice [the Justice Department] in Washington sittin' right there in front of the courthouse taking pictures, asking questions to see if anything had happened where they could report it back to Washington.

In two days, three of us got in: Mr. John Daniel Wesley, Mr. Turnbow second, and I was third. Well, that was unfair because you know what time the courthouse open in the mornin'. And we'd stay there until it close in the evenin', way over in the afternoon.

How many times did you go back?

RR: Five, and then they said that I didn't do anything right. I said, "Well, I know I did one thing—I wrote my name right." And they said, "Naw, weren't anything right."

I've read your interview done by your grandson, and it mentioned something in there about Reverend Trent.

RR: Reverend Trent was one of the black ministers of Lexington—he was pastoring on Highway 17—and when we came up from Mileston to redishter for the first day, Reverend Trent joined us. He lived in town. And so that night, by him being by hisself and didn't have anyone with him, the policeman got at him and told him he'd give him thirty minutes to get outta town. And he left. And he went through three counties 'fore he stopped: Carroll County and I think Leflore County and another

Applicants for Registration

Submitted for publication on May 5, 1964.

Rosebud Clark, Tchula, Miss.

Jodie Saffold, Jr., Durant, Miss.

Virginia Catrol Saffold, Durant, Miss.

Jodie Saffold, West, Miss.

Jesse J. Russell, Tchula, Miss.

Flora Howard, Tchula, Miss.

Cora Lee Roby, Durant, Miss

Andrew Jackson Butler, Durant, Miss.

Mary Alice Wright, West, Miss.

Vandbilt Roby, Durant, Miss.

Link Williams, Durant, Miss.

Ida Mae Williams, Durant, Miss.
5-7-2tc

FIGURE 2 *Left: from legal notices section in the* Holmes County Herald, *June 1964.* PHOTO, *right: farmer and fiery orator Hartman Turnbow was a Movement leader and a strong believer in armed self-defense. "The lynchings and killings frightened the Negroes and kept them scared, and for a long time," Mr. Turnbow explained to Movement volunteer and historian Sue Lorenzi. "But this now, this is something we is in together. So every time they come shooting or bombing, that just made us all mad and more determined to go on." (From Susan [Lorenzi] Sojourner, "The Holmes County Civil Rights Movement Participants: The Mood, Feel, Environment of 1963–1967," Paper to the Annual Meeting of the American Anthropological Association, 1985, p. 4.)*

county. They didn't hurt him because he outranned 'em. We found him later, but he didn't come back.

Why did they put the names in the newspaper of those who were tryin' to register?

RR: They did that to let the Ku Klux Klan and the Citizens' Council know who was in the group. They also took pictures and put them on the front line in publicity.

Could you tell us what they did to Mr. Turnbow?

RR: They bombed Mr. Turnbow's house, locked him up. They took the sashes outta his windows, and they killed his dog. This was while Turnbow was at one of our meetings. Then they hid down on the turn

The late Hartman Turnbow's home in Mileston.

row [a dirt track in the fields where tractors turn around], not too distant from his house.

I believe it was after two o'clock when they came. They threw firebombs into his livin' room and one in his other bedroom. Burned the sheets and his quilts and whatnots, and burned the livin' room out. One man was standing at the front door with his .45 and another was at the back waiting on Mr. Turnbow to come out with the intention of killing him and putting him back in the house 'til the house burned up.

But his wife and daughter ran outside. The whites didn't bother the wife and daughter. They rushed back in and tol' Mr. Turnbow, said, "Somebody out there." And Mr. Turnbow had a .22 sixteen-shooter rifle, and he went and got it. He come out, and the man standing—he aimed right in his stomach and shot, fired three times. And the man whirled and ran, and Turnbow steady shooting, the moon shinin' like day. He emptied that .22 rifle, and they all ran and went down 'n' put the one Mr. Turnbow hit in the car 'n' carried him on to the hospital.

Did Mr. Turnbow kill him?

RR: He died later, but they wouldn't own it. They say he had a heart attack.

Was Mr. Turnbow arrested for that?

RR: Well, they didn't arrest him for that because they wouldn't let that be known. That the first time a black man killed a white man in Mississippi, and they wouldn't own it. They knew it happened that way. In fact, it seems the sheriff, Andrew Smith, was with them. He lost his tag [license plate] down there by Turnbow's house on a turn row. I guess he took it off or dragged it off. It seems the sheriff and his men did it. They said the Ku Klux Klan, but the Citizens' Council were doing the same thing. I reckon all of 'em was members of both organizations.

Was the sheriff ever convicted for that?

RR: No, they didn't do anything to the sheriff. They bombed Mr. Turnbow's house around two o'clock in the mornin' and then locked him up.

You say they arrested him, but they didn't arrest him for killing the white man. What did they arrest him for?

RR: Because they say he was leading it. They bombed his house and said he bombed and burned his own house. And they charged him with arson. When we carried the sheriff to court, they lifted that arson charge offa Turnbow.

Didn't y'all also file a lawsuit against the circuit clerk?

RR: We carried them both down there [to the federal court in Jackson, Mississippi], the circuit clerk and the sheriff. We couldn't make out the affidavits against them in Lexington, 'cause the lawyer in Lexington wouldn't fix the papers. But we went out of town.

Were they ever convicted?

RR: He didn't serve no time, but we made him purge hisself for not allowing us to redishter to vote. I was in the courtroom listenin' to them lyin' witnesses for six days. He brought his friends in to clear him, to say he didn't keep us from redishterin' to vote. He had 'bout fifteen lying witnesses—all of 'em were white; they say he didn't do this, he didn't do that. They had old men, young men, middle-age men that were voting; they couldn't even write their name. But they was white. They were redishtered voters. And I asked the circuit clerk how that got to be. "I don't know." They knew how they got there; they just put their names on.

I was one of the material witnesses. He told me to get out of town, but I didn't go. I was gonna be the next eye witness; but when he saw me, he purged hisself and came out and shook hands with our leaders. I didn't testify against him because John Doar [an official of the U.S. Justice Department] say, "If you testify against him, Reverend Russell, they'll bust him and take his job from him. We got you here to make him behave."

Because in court, y'see, we had John Doar. And we had a lawyer representing us, Mr. Rosenberg, and also other lawyers from the Justice [Department] from Washington. That was the federal government. 'Cause the local government was training dogs to put on us when we'd go to the courthouse. They had a dog up there in Lexington, but they didn't bring him out the day we went up.

Before that, we had carried the high sheriff off to court for about three days before he would purge hisself from not lettin' us redishter to vote. And Mrs. Hazel Brannon Smith, she was one of the witnesses against the sheriff. She say he did say he wadn't gonna allow us to redishter long as he was sheriff. He denied it.

Who came down to help y'all get organized to register to vote?

RR: We had a young man called Bob Moses (he was our extension worker), Samuel Block, and John Ball from SNCC—also Mrs. Annell Ponder from SCLC.

Where were the citizenship classes held?

RR: We held them at the Mileston Church 'n' Jerusalem Church. Most of the churches was afraid. We held the classes in our homes, mostly Mr. Turnbow and Mr. Dave Howard, Ozell Mitchell, Sam Redmond, and my home. Then we got Jerusalem Church and we started holdin' classes there.

After that we got our Movement on the way. When we got someone registered, then we wrote a letter into Atlanta, to Dr. Martin Luther King and the Southern Christian Leadership Conference. Told 'em we had a Movement goin' on, but we didn't have any place to meet. And he told us to send in twenty-five dollars for a affiliatin' certificate, and we did that. They sent this letter to California, and California funded us with some money to build a center which is called the "Holmes County Community Center." And it's the first center that was built in Holmes County. We started meeting in our center from then on. It's still there.

Did y'all ever encounter any threats while you were having these classes?

RR: Yes, they would come by and harass the ones that would go to the center, give 'em tickets, and follow 'em. Come back and burned crosses— the Ku Klux Klan—and then they stop your cars and search them 'n' see what you had in there—any li'ture from Dr. Martin Luther King.

MR: The highway patrolmen—they didn't have any black patrolmen at that time—they would give illegal tickets to mostly everybody that was in the Movement. At that time, young folk and a very few elderly people participated. Everybody got harassed mostly, even me. The sheriff, the highway patrolmen, and police all get in one car and follow us right on up to the church and turn around. Sometimes they'd follow us home right to the fork and turn into our house. . . .

RR: Then they put their lights out and follow you, blacked out.

Did you ever have any passwords or things you had to do to keep yourself safe?

RR: Well, just with my wife. I would go to a meeting and come in at a certain time. I always had a password between her and me if I spoke, so she would know. Then I'd have a certain blow with my car horn. She'd know that it was me and don't turn no lights on.

You said you wouldn't turn on any lights in the car?

RR: Mmm hmm! We didn't turn any on—like the dashlights in the car. We took all them out. We didn't have nothing but headlights and taillights in the car. So when you come into the house, you didn't turn the lights on. You see, a sniper could be in the bushes and [laughs] bump you off if you would turn a light on.

Did they ever use violence against you?

RR: Yes, some of them did. They'd shoot in your houses. They burned one of my churches—Bell Chapel—down to the ground. Knocked out the window panes on the south side of West Shady Grove [Church], sashes 'n' everything; they knock the whole thang out. That was to stop us, but we didn't stop.

Was there a Citizens' Council located here in Lexington?

RR: Sure! They had 'bout twelve hundred members, were well organized. They didn't have a special building. They'd just meet in the courthouse or the city hall 'cause it wouldn't be no blacks with 'em. They could meet any time they got ready.

Do you think that most people feared 'cause of the things they did?

RR: Yes, 'cause they were shootin' people and burning crosses and harassing them and givin' 'em illegal tickets. And you go down the road—they search your car: "Where you going?" You had to talk.

Were many farmers ever denied loans because of their involvement in the Movement?

RR: We got our loans all right, but some places wouldn't gin the cotton, and some places they couldn't sell the cotton. They had to go out the county, or go to Jackson or some other place to sell the cotton.

Were you ever tempted to use violence against them for what they did?

RR: Naw, I didn't. Our Movement was nonviolent. *Nonviolence is a sword that cuts without wounding.* It's a sword that moves through cities and make people anew and leave buildings standin' and not burned down. We couldn't use violence.

Did you carry a gun?

RR: Never. My pistol, lemme show you my pistol. [Laughs as all the students crane their necks to see him reach into his briefcase.] I have a gun, and this is the gun I use. [Digs in his briefcase and holds up the Holy Bible.]

The Bible. . . .

RR: That's the best weapon of all times. When I get out, I pull it up. The policeman starts tremblin'—he have his pistol—'n' he goes to shaking. When I go in the courthouse, we would go in and carry the Bible. And they'd be shaking. They never did stop me on the road; they'd stop everybody but me. But they followed us at night with their lights out, and I'd lay my Bible right up on the dash. When they see that Bible, it just does something to them. There's something about this Bible that if you carry your Bible with you, you don't have to worry about anything. Ain't nobody gonna bother you.

What was the response of many other people after they found out you couldn't use violence, when they went out to march and violence was used against them? Did a lot of people drop out or did it encourage more to join?

RR: Well, we only had one person that probably would have used violence, but we didn't let him march. That was Mr. Turnbow. Now if you hit Mr. Turnbow or did something to him, you had to fight him. He just wouldn't take it. So he went along with us when we marched, but we told him not to march—just to stand on the side and look.

The first march was formed in Lexington. There was five hundred and fifty people, and you know by that we were well organized. We marched from Pecan Grove to up on the square without any trouble. We marched three hours around the courthouse, sang, prayed, and then talked to the town. That was our first march. White and black together, but it wasn't the local whites. Those from up North—Chicago, Detroit, Ohio, and everywhere. They came in to help us. We all held hands together and marched around.

What was the purpose of that march?

RR: We lettin' 'em know we were putting the spotlight on Lexington. We drilled our people before we came up to Lexington. Y'see, Holmes County was a bull with long horns goin' in the Movement. The way they was keeping us from going to the courthouse to redishter. Most folks was afraid. We marched, and we dehorned that bull, and he became a steer [laughs]. After you dehorned him, he can't do nothing. Following that march, we got more people to participate that was afraid. More than five hundred fifty was marchers, and the rest of the streets was full 'cause they hadn't never seen nothing like that before. So the march was a success.

What was the response of the white community?

RR: Well, it soften them up and let them know that we were nonviolent and we didn't mean to fight, but we just want to exercise our right and privilege to redishter to vote.

What role did the women play in the Civil Rights Movement?

RR: They worked along with the men. The women were right there. We had several women in there when we tried to register that first time: Mrs. Rosebud Clark, Mrs. Nancy Epps, Mrs. Alma Carnegie, Mrs. Annie Bell Mitchell, Flora Howard, Jessie Mae Howard, and Mrs. Clark had her little boy, James, there—'bout two years old.

MR: The women were behind them all. Some were teachin' classes; some were going off on workshops in South Carolina. And they had to have feeding programs. There was a time when they had to have babysitters for the ones that had to go up to redishter to vote. Some women had to babysit those children and volunteered to do all of this. Everything that was done at that time was volunteer: No one got paid for anything.

RR: We picked cotton for two dollars and fifty cents a hundred [pounds] and put gas in the car. And every Sunday morning we was out in another community where the Movement wadn't organized, 'n' recruited people, talking at the churches. And that's how we did it—with our own money. An' I taught classes at Mount Olive and Holly Grove and also at Mileston and other precincts. And the money we raise—I would give it to the treasurer. An' that's how we did it.

Did you have any freedom riders stay with you? ["Freedom riders" is a generic term used by Holmes Countians to refer to outside activists and volunteers.]

RR: Yes, we had a summer project in 1964, and I went up to Oxford, Ohio, to the orientation program; and there were 'bout two thousand [students] there when we orientated them to come here in Mississippi for the first summer project. Black and white came from there. They help us to canvass, going around knockin' on everybody's door to follow us. Y'see, people didn't know 'bout the Movement, and they was afraid. And we had to go and visit them. 'S called canvassin'. And they help us do that. Some were black; some are doctors, lawyers, nurses, and you name it.

Did they have trouble adjusting to life down here?

RR: Not much because we tol' them the role of Mississippi 'n' what they would run into when we went up there. A busload of us went for about a week. And we tol' 'em what would happen when they be here, and they were willin' to come. Because we told 'em that's a black community, Mileston, down there, where over two hundred families own their own land. And we controls that. Black folks! Got their own stores, got the co-op. We had a [cotton] gin, but we don't have it now. So that's how we were able to go alone. And the police wouldn't come down in there and take over, like they do in town. And we told 'em that's where they'd be staying, most of 'em in our homes.

You said that you and some others went up to Ohio to help with the orientation for the summer project in 1964. Were you up there when they heard about Goodman, Chaney and Schwerner being killed? What were the response of the other volunteers when they heard about this at the meeting?

RR: They was more willing to come help after. When they found out that they was gonna be livin' with us an' we'd protect 'em. 'Cause when you're comin' into my home, ain't nobody comin' in there an' take over 'n' get nobody out, if you get in my house. The sheriff don't get in unless he read a warrant. He ain't comin' in. And that's how it is. An' all the peoples in the Mileston area is situated like that—they own from sixty-five acres up to two hundred. I have sixty-five, and it's mine; and nobody comes in there and gets on there unlessen they see me.

The sheriff sent somebody down to investigate, but he sit on down 'n' talk with me an' says, "Reverend Russell," he says, "Now we don't mind y'all registerin' to vote, but we don't want your boys and gals courtin' our white gals and like that."

I said, "Do you think that's the cause of it?"

He said, "No."

"Well," I said, "You shut your mouth up on that!" I said, "Now if you down here and you come in shinin' lights in these folks' houses and barns like you's looking for convicts, you can tell the sheriff I said to stay away from down 'ere. If he don't, he goin' to get killed. I'm not gonna kill him," I said. "But everybody's ready." He reached out and shook ma hand.

How did the local whites respond to Freedom Summer?

MR: They didn't seem to like it too well because the whites [the volunteers from the North] and blacks cooperated real well. And the young ladies and young men 'n' all worked together real good. This is what the white and black didn't do in our own community. White girls and black boys just didn't work together and have any association with each other.

And you had to say "Yes ma'm" and "No ma'm" and "No sir" to everybody, whether they were adult people or boy or girl?

RR: If you didn't say it, you get in trouble. So we broke that up. Now you can say "Yes" and "No" to [laughs] anybody. Now it's an honor to say "Sir" to folks in office or in the army. And they had a habit of callin' you "Boy"—didn't care if you were seventy years old. And "Auntie" and "Uncle" [laughs]. That was the custom. And they call most of the black folks "niggers." We broke that up. That was a lowdown hated race name. I hate to say the word. And some of our folks don't know no better. We want to cancel that word from our vocabulary.

What were the consequences of the Movement?

MR: During that time there were people that could not read and write, and we had classes. Those people learned how to read, write, how to write checks, how to bank money, and how to get money outta the bank. People didn't know how to just take care of their own business. All of this they learned in the Movement.

Some of the consequences were learnin' how to live and get along together with other races—not just with white races but anybody. You all had to cooperate together to get what we got now. So the Movement led us up to young black boys and girls gettin' jobs at early ages, gettin' jobs in stores, in schools, and places they had never worked before. They didn't have that advantage then. We had separate water fountains; we had separate seats on buses, in the doctor's office and places like that. We all sit together now, wherever we can find a seat.

RR: When you go to the place where they auction off the livestock, they had a place where you eat there. You couldn't go in there and eat with the buyers. You had to go to a hole in the wall there, where they reach your food out to you if you eat. That's the way it was.

We couldn't use the school for anything. We couldn't use the City Hall in Lexington. Couldn't use the Town Hall of Tchula. We had to meet in our homes or somewhere else.

And may I add that we did not have the Head Start daycare, what we have for the children. That came through the Movement. We sent representatives to Washington and asked for the Head Start—and here it come through the Movement.

Did that make you feel proud of what you had done?

RR: Sure! It does something to me when I hear tell of somebody elected in our state or county, and 'specially when we go to Washington—like our senators and our congressmen. It excites me when I hear that. An' like Mrs. Banks of Tchula that was elected the mayor and Eddie James Carthan, our first mayor. We didn't have blacks that active in Holmes

County. We didn't have deputies, and now our sheriff is black. And we didn't have the black superintendent. And we put the state representative, Robert Clark. Had to stay up late to do it, but we did it.

Mr. Love was the representative at that time. Clark won out, but they had one of the boxes they put the votes in, 'n' they brang it to Tchula and fill that box up with votes. Then that box would disappear before they count it. An' we stood in there and tole 'em: "Don't move that box!"

And them votes what was in that box—they was gonna do away with 'em and take out what they wanted, and Representative Clark probably would not ha' gotten it. But they didn't move that box, and we counted all those votes, and he got in there.

Did y'all ever witness anybody ever being killed or lynched or anything like that?

MR: Injured but not killed in Holmes County. In other places people got killed, but in Holmes County they got injured; people got shot.

Were you ever afraid for your safety while you was in the Movement?

RR: No, I wadn't. I didn't have time to be afraid. When I hear tell of we gonna have a meeting somewhere, I couldn't sleep because I wanted to be there [laughs]. I's worked like Dr. Martin Luther King. They used to call me in Holmes County the second Martin Luther King, because it was danger here just like it was down there. I wadn't a bit more afraid of nothin'.

Mrs. Russell, did you ever fear for him being in the Movement?

MR: Oooh, yes. . . .

RR: [Laughs].

MR: The children and I would sit up until twelve and one o'clock at night watching our home, because our home was the third one on the list to be bombed. We would sit up watching the house, and then he would get up sometime and sit up the rest of the night.

But when he had to travel at night, I was at home because we had 'bout eleven children at home at that time. I had twelve, 'n' one was away in school. So we would watch the house while he was away. But I was always lookin' for him [to come] in at a certain time.

If they was ever runnin' late, we would get uneasy. Sometime they would kinda run late, 'cause people had bad cars then; they didn't have good cars like we have now. They had the kinda cars that would break down on the road. They had to fix that car before they could get in, and they'd maybe run a little late. Yeeeeees, I was afraid for his safety.

How did you overcome that fear?

MR: We didn't really overcome that fear until everybody seem to get together and cooperate together and work together. *Many peoples was afraid in the beginning and they stayed afraid, afraid as they can get. But there was some that just wasn't afraid to continue because we was tryin' to reach a goal—something not just for ourselves but for everybody.* And we had to continue to work to get somewhere. It was dangerous, but you don't stop; you go on anyway—that's just how it is.

RR: It wadn't easy. People don't know what it cost to get this. But I say this: We gotta work harder to keep this than we did to get it. An' our young people like you gotta be educated to this, what we did. Just like y'all doing. It wadn't easy.

MS. AUSTRY KIRKLIN

"That Was a White Man's World"

LEKESHIA BROOKS & TELESHIA KIRKLIN

Ms. Austry Kirklin was born on March 26, 1935. She attended the Little Red Schoolhouse that was set up by the Freedmen's Bureau after the Civil War. Ms. Kirklin has picked cotton on a plantation almost half her life, beginning at the age of twelve. She is the mother of ten children. Three different cultures—Indian, African, and white—flow together to make up her bloodlines. Her mother was half Indian and half African. Her daddy was a mixture of African and white. Her grandmother, a full-blooded Indian, could wrap her hair around her neck three times.

Ms. Kirklin looks younger than her fifty-four years. She has a bright facial color. She talks fast, but you can understand her. When she speaks, she sometimes moves her hands to better express what she's saying. She is a church-going person. When you ask her to come to your church, she is more than willing to come, even if you don't go to hers.

Ms. Kirklin has a lot of courage, but she also has sense. When she marched in Jackson and the police began to beat on people, she locked herself in a bathroom with a friend. She believes strongly in what she does. And she's still involved in the Movement. For the past ten years, she has volunteered at the Rural Organizing and Cultural Center, helping to run the used-clothing store. She loves to talk about the Civil Rights Movement because she wants us to know how she struggled so that our lives might be easier than hers.

Ms. Kirklin is our grandmother, and we're glad of that because she's the nicest and most caring person we know. We love her, and we will always be proud of her accomplishments in the Movement.

[In the following interview, **AK** is Ms. Austry Kirklin.]

Why did you get started in the Movement?

AK: I got started in the Movement because things wadn't going to suit us in Holmes County. And a group of peoples got together and tried to do somethin' about it.

What things?

AK: Just like the white people, and the schools was not desegregated. And when we got ready to vote 'n' all, they didn't allow no black peoples to have no voice in nothin'. They always wanted the white person to have a voice in it.

What things needed changing?

AK: The schools, the jobs. The whole system needed changing.

What made you want to participate in all this?

AK: I wanted to better my condition. I didn't like how things was going, and I didn't want my children brought up like I was.

And just like they killed Emmett Till in 1955. They maintained he had whistled at a white girl or did somethin' at a white girl, and they killed him. Cut part of his limbs off and threw him in a creek. He had come down to visit his grandmother that summer. I felt real bad about it because I had children of my own. And I know how his mother felt about him. Everybody felt real bad. They would have killed some more black peoples' children. We was tryin' to let 'em know we didn't like it.

What did they do to keep you down in Holmes County?

AK: They didn't give black people no really good jobs. Back then they didn't let black people vote; they kept them out. White power had all the vote. If you stayed on a plantation or somethin', your bossman wadn't gonna let you register to vote. The sheriff believe what the plantation man say. If something happen and the bossman didn't call the sheriff, he didn't come. And you didn't have no other alternative. White people ruled the county.

What made you all of a sudden just start the Movement? How come you didn't start it before?

AK: We really didn't know no better before. And somebody came out and talked us into it and showed us that we could live better. You ain't got to live in them old shack houses on them white folks' place. You ain't gotta chop that cotton for two dollars a day. And we wanted to do better for ourself.

Way back, when you got ready to go get the commodities, some groceries that they would be giving out, the bossman had you up in a cotton truck like you was a cow. And they would say, "My Negroes gotta go to the field. I want them to hurry up and be served." And they wait on all us, and you get in that truck and go on home. I hated the way we had to live. We had a miserable life.

Back then, didn't have no running water, no inside bathroom, no refrigerator, no electric lights. The white people had all kinds of convenience. They should've had it, 'cause they worked us to death for nothing. Didn't give us nothing but two dollars a day. And took all the money when you made a crop. You made fifty bales of cotton, you didn't clear nothin'. Say, "You'll do better next year."

Black people made white people rich. That's the reason the white man didn't want the black person to vote. 'Cause they know they had lost their power. After we voted, they knew we was gon' do better. So they kept us in the dark long as they could.

Were the blacks the ones that kept the whites in power, by working for them?

AK: The blacks really kept the whites going 'cause the whites didn't do nothing. We worked for 'em, cleaned the house, cooked for 'em. They didn't give us nothing. But we didn't have no other choice. And the white person got rich off us. The way the white person worked us, they should be richer than what they are.

Was there a point in your life when you wanted to stop and overthrow the whites?

AK: It was a point in my life when I was working for this old white lady. She must have been mad when I got there that morning. It was a younger white lady there, and I was dusting.

She told this young white lady, "Ooh, my Lord, I ain't never ate nothing behind a black nigger." And I was listening right at her. But the young white lady just looked at me; she didn't say nothing. So the old white lady said it again, "Oh, my Lord, I ain't never ate nothing behind a black nigger."

And I just kept on dusting; I didn't say a word to her. So, 'bout that time I cooked her dinner. She was already mad. She came through there in her wheelchair and jumped up in my collar and grabbed me. She said, "Oh, my Lord, you black son of a bitch, you nigger, if you had been on [as hired help] way back in the '30s, I'd take a stick of stove wood and beat the hell outta you."

What did you do then?

AK: I got mad, grabbed that lady, shook her, turned her a'loose, and sent her upside the wall. Her eyes got big. And she called all her brother-in-laws and her daughter and her grandson in.

An' I worked for her about two more weeks, and I quit 'cause I was gonna kill that lady. She was gonna make me kill her. And that's what really made me stop working for white folk.

When I quit working for her, then I started workin' for Miss Maureen Blaylock at a cleaners. Then 'bout '67 I started working at Durant Sportswear where mighty few blacks worked. You had to work hard and strong to stay there.

Y'see, way back, white people use' to whip black people if you didn't go to the field on time. They'd whip you. And weren't nothing you could do. You had to go to the field from sunup 'til sundown.

What did they pay you?

AK: Two dollars a day. All day long. And Friday you couldn't quit to wash. You had to keep on in the field. If some of your people died, the only way you got to go to the funeral, you had to ask your bossman. 'Cording how he felt about it.

And way back in the '60s Mrs. Mae Catherine Falls whooped Mr. Willie Joe Waites. He had a walking stick, and he came up there and say, "Everybody else in the field. I want you to go to the field. Your mama didn't raise you like this."

She say, "Mr. Waites, you ain't none of my damn daddy. I ain't got no goddamn white daddy." Mr. Waites got out like he gonna hit at her with a walking stick, and she got that stick and beat him nearly to death. He left there runnin'. Run off and left his truck. She was the only black woman ever whooped a white man back in the '60s. She left, went on down to her mama's house. She left his plantation.

When did you register to vote?

AK: 'Bout '63 or '64. When we went up to try to register to vote, they would threaten ya. The sheriff had that German Shepherd dog—tried to turn that dog aloose on you in the yard. Let him run up 'side you and scare you and pull him back. We had a hard time. We went up there about three times. They would threaten you if you go up alone. They said black peoples wadn't allowed to vote. That was a white man's world.

What did you do then?

AK: Just stand there along with Edgar Love—he was kinda bad then—and Old Man Sims. Mr. [William] Sims carried that .45 with him. He wadn't scared of nothing. Stand there and say, "We demand we are going to register to vote."

How did you feel in the office?

AK: Felt good for trying to vote. I knowed it was dangerous, but we still felt good. 'Cause if we had the power to vote, we could do more thangs with the town. We had a little power o'er who get in the office.

When you'd get in there, he'd ask you, "Can you read? What's your mother's name?" Or, "Who did this and that?" Try to throw you off the track. If you couldn't do this and that, they didn't want you to vote.

But then the federal man came down. He said that if you couldn't read and write, make the "X" and you still could vote. 'Cause they had passed the Voting Rights Act.

Did anyone try and get at you for registering?

AK: No, I wasn't threatened 'cause I wadn't on no plantation. And I wadn't workin' for no white person. I was livin' on Ulysses Lewis's place, workin' in the field then.

Did the whites ask him to fire you?

AK: They never did ask him 'cause he was black. But if I had been livin' on the plantation, they would have. But later on down the line— since I'm at ROCC—I was workin' for a white lady. And one day she saw me passing out fliers with Sister Louise. And so that night she called me up and told me she couldn't use me no more 'cause her money had ranned out. She just saw me working with the Sisters.

What type of meetings did you go to in the '60s?

AK: We went to meetings in a little house in the Pecan Grove, called the FDP meeting. And we gotten together and participated, and discussed how we was gonna perform our march and things. Sometimes in the schoolhouse, the House of Clark, churches, different places.

We sang, we prayed, then we talked about how we was goin' to march. We met secretly and talked about what we was gonna do. Because the white people was always tryin' to surprise the black. So we had a surprise for them. We didn't want them to know what we was gettin' into until we was ready to do it.

What do you think they would have done if they had found out what you all were doing?

AK: I think the peoples what had jobs, they'd threaten 'em 'bout, "We gonna fire you." Those peoples on a plantation, white people made 'em move. The Ku Klux Klan would ride by at night and burn a cross in your yard. They called at night and threatened to burn your house down.

Did you recognize any of the people who threatened you?

AK: No, I didn't because they had those white sheets on; you could just see the eyes—you couldn't recognize 'em.

Did the sheriff do anything about it?

AK: The sheriff didn't do nothing about it. Old Man Andrew Smith was rough back then.

Edgar Love, Eugene Montgomery, Pat Henson, and SNCC volunteers confront (from left) Deputy Sheriff Billy Joe Gilmore, Sheriff Andrew P. Smith, and a Lexington policeman at City Hall in July 1967 over instances of police brutality.

I remember when a man called Meter Mack was the police. He shot a black man down on Beale Street in cold blood. The police shot him down that Saturday evening; he was in the cafe talkin' to some womens. I walked right over him, A. W. Brown's daddy. The city police, Meter Mack, shot him and killed him. For no reason.

'Course, they made somethin' up about how the man had threatened the police, and he had to shoot him. Self-defense—that's what they put out. But they always put out something that ain't true.

How did they make you feel when they shot him?

AK: We got kinda scared and went on down the street and got in our car and went home.

Around Freedom Summer in 1964, did you know about the three civil rights workers who were killed?

AK: Yes, I did. They came down to help out and then got put in jail in Philadelphia. [The killers] went to the jailhouse and got 'em about twelve o'clock that night and killed 'em. Dug a hole with a bulldozer

Rev. Seymour speaks with Henry Lorenzi at the FDP office in the Pecan Grove neighborhood of Lexington in early 1965. Mr. Lorenzi and his wife Sue worked as volunteers with the local Movement from 1964 through 1969.

and buried 'em over in a pasture somewhere and covered 'em back up. Even the sheriff of that town knew. I think that he was a part of it.

Did that make the white volunteers afraid to come down here?

AK: They was more willing to come and do whatever they could to better Holmes County and around.

How did the local whites respond to the Movement?

AK: Quite naturally, local white peoples got mad 'cause they been havin' their way all the time. They knew that if black peoples gotten the chance to vote, that was gonna cut their power off. When the Movement start, the only whites we had to join our marches was the whites outta town— none of the white residents in Holmes County. But I remember we was marching up on Beale Street and the Ku Klux Klan was marching down by Mr. Quick's.

How would the White Citizens' Council or the Ku Klux Klan try to hurt you?

AK: They had rock throwing 'n' all. The white people cursed and said numerous things. But we marched anyway. It was a large number of us marching, and that makes a difference. Then the white people'd get mad and try to get into their trucks and run up in the march. But we would always look out for that. We always kept the mens to protect. They run on our side, protect you, and tried to keep track of everything in the march. We was nonviolent. Nobody never did fight back. Mr. Sims, he used to always carry his gun—him and Joe Smith.

Then we would do boycotts, y' know, to try and solve the problem. Punish the merchandiser. We kept that dollar in our pocket, and they'll try to straighten up and fly right.

Were you involved in the march in Jackson, where they beat people and then jailed them in animal stables at the fairgrounds?

AK: Yes, I went down, but when they started to beatin' 'em over their head and put that water hose on ya, put them dogs on ya, Lillie Ree Gibson and myself, we went into a bathroom and locked up. They beat 'em and jailed a lot of 'em. They jailed Mr. [William] Sims down there. Kept him three weeks when they found he had a gun. But we was lucky; we was not jailed.

Who all was involved with you in the Movement?

AK: Myself, Ms. Lela Mae Walden, Ms. Lucille Mitchell, Mary Hightower, Georgia Clark, Marie Fisher, Tack Hooker, an' Sue and Harriet from Washington, D.C.—they was some white people to help us. I could just go on and on.

Most of the people you were involved with, were they women?

AK: Majority was womens. Mens was small: Edgar Love, Joe Smith, Reverend Warren G. Booker, T. C. Johnson, Mr. Walter Johnson. . . .

Did the men treat you as equals?

AK: Yeah, they treat us all the same.

Were they ever afraid for you? Did they try to stop you from marching or anything like that?

AK: No, they never did try to stop us. We just kept on marching right on up to Freedom Lane and sang that song "Keep on Getting Up."

How did the women defend themselves against the Ku Klux Klan or someone who was to come by their house at night? What did they do, like if their husband was gone?

AK: See, they'd warn ya. They'd burn a cross in your yard. And if they call you and threaten you, a lot of men would just come, stayed with the guns that night. An' if they come back, shooting and goin' on, they'd try to scare 'em away.

Were there any blacks who tried to talk you out of being involved in the Movement?

AK: Yeah, a lot of them black people say, "Chile, you gonna get killed, If I was you, I wouldn't go off and leave my children like that. They gonna kill you."

Our bossman tol' us, "Don't mess with them civil rights folk. They ain't nothing but trouble."

And right now they call me a troublemaker 'cause I got involved and I been in there ever since. I still know a few people live on plantations say, "Chile, you gonna get killed. You just follow them old white folk. You just follow." Now they say, "You gonna get killed 'cause you follow them old nuns. Them old nuns ain't nothing but communists and troublemakers."

Y'all first really started the Movement in Holmes County—set the pace and got everything goin'—then others joined in after. How did you feel about that?

AK: I felt good. After we got in, then they see they didn't do anything to us. And then we could encourage somebody else to come 'n' join us.

I been marching a long time. They never did do nothing to me. All my children's safe. And marched and marched and we didn't get hurt.

We encouraged some of them on plantations to march. But the white people made 'em move after they was in the march. Black people had to run off over night. They had to leave their hogs, their cows, or whatever they had, 'cause they didn't allow you to get nothing.

Did any stay?

AK: A few stayed. But the majority of 'em found a brighter light— they went to bigger cities.

What do you think things would be like today if you hadn't gotten involved in the Movement—you and everybody that started it?

AK: I think we would've been back in slavery. Sometimes after we did all that strugglin', they still think you in slavery. They don't want you to have no voice. They think black people are not capable of handling no government job. Today black people are capable of handling anything better than a white man.

If you had to do it all over again, would you join the Movement?

AK: I'd do it all over again. And I would try to encourage that many more: young and old, crippled, white, black, poor white—don't make no difference, creed or color.

Did the thought of getting killed ever scare you?

AK: It didn't scare me one bit. I say, "Lord, if I get killed trying to better my condition, somebody else gon' carry it on."

MRS. CORA LEE ROBY & MR. VANDERBILT ROBY

"Stickin' the Best We Can"

MARQUES SAFFOLD

Mrs. Cora Lee and Mr. Vanderbilt Roby are one of the nicest couples around. They were both born near the Old Pilgrim Rest community, where they live now. My first memories of them are from church, when they would give me peppermint candy. And every time I'd go to their house with my grandmother, Mrs. Roby would offer me a snack as soon as I'd walk in the door.

Mr. Vanderbilt is a tall, lanky man who always wears a hat. He raised cattle and farmed for a living. Mr. Vanderbilt is known for his courage. "I's not scared of anybody," he told us. Mrs. Cora Lee is a short, warm, and gentle woman. Before she finished the eighth grade, she began teaching grammar school in her community.

Both Robys were active in the Civil Rights Movement. Because they are old, I didn't expect them to remember the exact details about the Movement. But Mrs. Roby told her stories as if they had happened yesterday. She was an important witness when the federal government took Henry McClellan to court for not allowing blacks to register to vote.

The couple was one of the few families in the community to join the Movement early on. Freedom riders stayed with them during the summer of '64. The Ku Klux Klan burned a cross in their yard to scare them into giving up. But the Robys kept fighting for our freedom, and I feel a mixture of pride, thankfulness, and hope when I think of how they struggled for all of us.

[In the following interview, the speakers are Mrs. Cora Roby (**CR**) and Mr. Vanderbilt Roby (**VR**).]

Could you tell me where you was born?

CR: I was born in Holmes County, 'bout a mile from where I'm livin', in the Old Pilgrim Rest community.

When was you born?

CR: September 24, 1906. There was four of us. I'm the only one livin'. I had a sister older, and then I was next. And then my brother and my baby sister.

Did you have your own children?

CR: I only had one chile, and that was a miscarry. I didn't have no chillun.

Did your daddy own his own land?

CR: When my father was able to buy some land, I was at least sixteen years old. We lived on a white man plantation.

Tenants?

CR: That's right, tenants. We was doing halves. And my father would draw money each month. They would furnish a family wid 'bout five chillun no more than 'bout ten dollars. Larger families may get fifteen. An' you drawed that every month as long as you was farmin'. But when you laid a crop by, you wouldn't get nothin'. About July 4th, you'd lay the crop by, and then they quit furnishin' 'til it time to gather. And my father and mother and us, when we got big 'nough to, we'd pick a bale of cotton and carry it to the gin.

If you's workin' on halves, you get half of the seed money, which weren't much like it is now. And on thirds, you get a third of the seed money. An' some peoples was able to rent; they was able to buy 'em a mule and maybe a plow. That renter could gather his crop in 'n' sell it wherever and pay that rent. I don't know how much the rent used to be. I reckon 'cordin' to how many acres you on.

Sharecroppin', the man get half of what you sell. It's his land and his material that you work with. And he get half of what you make. An' that farmer keep the other half. But now he's furnishin' the money, 'n' you had to pay that man back outta your half, and you had little or none left. And sometimes they had a bad crop year, and my father was lucky if he were able to get all of us a pair of shoes around. If those shoes wear out, you don't get no more; we be barefooted 'til the next crop. Same way with books.

I ain't finish the eighth grade. That was as far as it went. You could finish the twelfth grade if you in Lexington. I finished the seventh in the room [the one-room school at Old Pilgrim Rest]. But I went to Lexington to go to high school. I had almost completed the eighth grade, and I took the flu and had to come home. And I didn't go back then.

I probably would've went back, but the man [whose] plantation we was living on said, "Cora, it seem you been a good girl. Up there where

I live, they don't have no schooling for y'all. The nearest schooling is almost five miles, and the little children can't get to school."

He say [to my father], "I'll take her 'fore the superintendent, and if you let her teach school over there, I would hope she could get the job." My father agreed. And I went before the superintendent and he gave me the register, the book they keep the chilluns' names in. I taught there for two years. I hadn't quite finished eighth grade and that's when I married. My husband didn't want me to teach. And I stopped, which I oughtta been taught more. Me and him couldn't agree at all. So I left him. Then I started to summer school. You'd go to Durant to their high school, and go there for three weeks in summer school. That's what I 'tended for the two years that I was teaching.

After that, I didn't go to any more school until in '64, when the civil rights people come in here. I think it must've began down there by Tchula 'cause a man by the name of Ralthus Hayes would come out to the church every Sunday and teach us citizenship.

When the civil rights peoples came in, we didn't have no running water. Back then people had to walk some two miles to get the mail. The ice-maker wasn't runnin' then but every two weeks. Anyhow, they finally brought the lights here, and then we could buy a new 'frigerator. And nobody had no runnin' water. And we decided we would dig that spring out and buy a pump and could get a bathtub and cold water to the house. So we had runnin' water. We was the only coloreds then had running water.

In '64, when the civil rights folk come, I had a girl from Minneapolis and I had one girl from Chicago. And my brother had two boys, one from Chicago and the other boy is from California. And they would all come from Preacher Saffold's there to take a bath.

Well, the white peoples got so mad. I had a big old tree before the house got burned up. Those white girls and other white children would be by that tree, laughing and talking, and the white folks drive along here, cars we ain't hardly ever seed before. My husband left out the house, they kept an eye on him 'cross the road. They would stay behind those bushes sometimes most all night. He said if they had started shooting, he were gonna start shooting, too. But they didn't bother us.

That was the summer of '64, Freedom Summer, when they had the civil rights workers come down?

CR: That's right. At first we started redishin' [registering] to vote. An' the white peoples had never let no Negro redish here in Mississippi, that I know of. And so we went down to the courthouse. They had said they wadn't gonna let you sit on the courthouse square—it were trampling the grass down. I went twice, and every time Mr. McClellan turned me down; he was our circuit clerk then. "What's with you?"

I said, "I want to try and fill out an application so I can be able to redish to vote."

Well, the first time he said, "What do you want, some commodities?" I said, "No sir, I want an application; I want to try and fill it out so I'll be able to redish to vote."

"Here, you take it and you go back there in that room." So I took it and went back in that room. He walk up on us and said, "I don't want no talking back there." So I went back again and I fill it out the best I can; passed it to him. "Well, you can come back in three weeks, and then you'll know whether you passed or not." So three weeks later I went back. "What's for you?"

I said, "I come back to see whether or not I passed that test on the application."

"No!"

I said, "Could I have another blank?"

He said, "All right, do it right." And I went back in three weeks, and he told me no, I didn't pass. And I aksed him for another form, and he gave it to me and I filled it out. Time came round for me to go back there—the third time; I failed the third time.

It was one Sunday and they was having my uncle's funeral, and somebody came into church and told me, "Somebody's there wanna see ya."

And I done went out there, and the car was parked out in the road, and two white gentlemen got out, opened the door, gave me a seat in the car. That's when the one man say, "Sit down. See this," and gave me a piece of newspaper. That white gentleman said, "What does that mean?"

I read it and said, "Meant what it said. If what it said is true, they'd passed a law that the city policeman can go out on the highway. I guess it meant that they had the privilege to go out there and arrest peoples or, if not arrest, charge 'em for false speeding or something."

He aksed, as soon as we broke up, "Could we go to your home and talk with you?"

I say, "Yeah, you're welcome to go home with me if you wanna talk." So we come on home and they trail us on.

And I give 'em a seat and they sit down and they say, "Miss Roby, we seed where you had been through McClellan's office to pass the test the third time, and he said you didn't pass. What did he tell you?" They must have checked the courthouse or something. So I told them. And they say, "Well, we got you subpoenaed. Why don't you come down to

Jackson? Be there 'bout eight o'clock, Wednesday morning. We have filed a suit against McClellan. We want you to testify."

So I hated it awful bad to do it, but I told 'em I would. And John Allen Wright was subpoenaed too. So Wednesday morning we went, and when we got to the courthouse in Jackson, Mississippi, I was waiting for my—now y'all have to pardon me and excuse me for backing up—but who came here that Sunday, was Katzenbach. He was from Washington, lawyer an' that [Nicholas Katzenbach was U.S. Deputy Attorney General]. And when I got to Jackson, I was kinda afraid, but when I saw him I felt a little better. I had to go back that Thursday and Friday morning. And they didn't come. See, they kept all the witnesses separate so we couldn't hear how others testified. And finally they come down and called me, and I take a chair up there.

McClellan's lawyer was from Lexington. He aksed about the county I lived in. And aksed me how long had I been livin' in Holmes County. Told him, "All my life 'cept a few months I went up North."

And so he aksed me, "When you went to McClellan's office and aksed him for an application, did he tell you, 'Here and hurry up and get through with it'?"

I said, "No, he didn't."

He said, "Well, what did he say when you passed it in?"

I said, "He told me to come back in three weeks, when I would hear if I'd passed."

"No further questions."

Then he sat down and Mr. Katzenbach aksed me everything about the town and where I lived. And then he handed me two pieces of paper and he say, "Is this your handwriting?"

And I said, "Yes, it is!" Them was the applications I had filled out over there. And he took 'em back.

And he said, "I see on this last application, the last question he aksed you, it said Mississippi has a right to abide by her own law and happenings." And I didn't answer that question; I didn't put nothing there. He said, "What was meant; what did you think about that question?"

I said, "I thought Mississippi had a right to abide by the laws of the United States."

He said, "Mmm. Why's you didn't answer this?"

I said, "I was afraid Mr. McClellan would be mad."

He [Mr. Katzenbach] said, "No further questions" and took those applications.

Then I went back home. And when three weeks was up, I went back and I filled that application and passed it on. And from then on he passed every application that went in there, because John Allen Wright went in there and he say he was so upset he couldn't spell "Mississippi."

Really, he didn't know how to spell it, and then he passed him. He passed him; he didn't turn none of them down.

You was scared going down to Jackson?

CR: Yes, I was scared with the civil rights boy from California. I was scared to answer that question. I was 'fraid these white people would try to do something to him and me. They didn't care if it was murder. They might burn a mob cross and get peoples and take 'em out in the woods. They killed some.

This man was working on a plantation and talked back at the bossman. He ran outta the field and down in the woods and made it home. And t'say them white peoples come there and told his wife, they say, "Lillie, tell him to come out, see. We won't bother him, we just want to talk to him." And she told him to come out and see what they want.

They took him and carried him off in the woods, leavin' him paralyzed. He never was able to walk anymore. He died. I don't know what become of his wife and children. I think they moved North, but he died. And that there will make you afraid of white people.

Now, some Negroes never was afraid 'cause they got their reason and fight back, but sometimes you wouldn't have the opportunity to fight back. And I never wanted nothing like this to happen to me nor my husband, and so I was 'fraid. And I feel like all that's planned come from the Lord.

[Mr. Vanderbilt Roby drives up in his old Chevrolet pickup truck and joins us on the porch.]

Your wife has been telling us about the Movement in '64, and I was wondering if they started that White Citizens' Council to scare people like yourselves who was taking a stand. Did they ever try and fire your kin from their job, or not give them a loan or mess with your mortgage on your house, or anything like that?

VR: No, they never did that, but they done everything else but. I had this house up here on my other place. The boy called Fletch what stayed there wouldn't pay me. And he told me to come up there and he'd pay me. When I got up there that morning, I aksed the mother where was he, and she had pointed that he were in the house. I said okay, and they had left the door open there.

One mind said don't go in there. Happened I looked through the crack and there he stood behind the door with a great big stick, waitin' till I come in; then he was gonna hit me. And I just grabbed hol' to the knob of the door and pulled it to me and slammed it 'gainst him and jumped out there in front of him. When he run into me, I hit him.

He was young, but I was as much man as he was. And I fought him down on the bed and I hit a couple of licks. And he hollered, "Mama, mama, get him!" I hit him again, and he fell across the bed.

I walked on out. I said, "I ain't comin' up for no trouble; you owed me, and you had me to come up here. Don't you *never* mess with me no more." And he waited 'til I got near 'bout to the car and he come down there with an ax. I said, "If you come down here, I'll kill you. Just make a couple more steps." And he turned on back.

Now, some white folks, they had a store up there and they told him, said, "Put the law on him!" And Andrew Smith (he was the law at that time), he told a lie; he say that I'd throwed a gun on Fletch and beaten him up, but I didn't. Didn't have a gun. Well, I had a gun, but it was down there to my car. I didn't need no gun to whoop him.

Andrew Smith give that boy part to make out an affidavit against me. Andrew Smith was the high sheriff then. He was mean. He didn't play mean; he was sho' 'nough mean.

I made up my mind to go to town and carry some hogs. I had about six hogs, nice shoats. I got about a mile, the law overtaken me. It happened I didn't have no gun, and as he slowed me down, I stopped. He say, "I got a writ against you. This here boy say you throwed a gun on him and beat him up."

I say, "I ain't a bit more throwed no gun on that boy than I throwed one on you. But I didn't have to throw no gun on him to whoop him."

And he say, "Well I'm just doing my job; gonna have to take you to jail." I call my wife, I told her go get my brother-in-law to come and bond me out.

It was, I say, 'bout two months later I had my trial. And I had my lawyers in there—civil rights lawyers. Andrew Smith and them didn't know, but I had two of them. And so they brought me, Fletch, and his mother and little sister. The high sheriff carried them in another room. I don't know what he say to them.

Fletch was a colored fellow. They was using him because I had these white [civil rights] folks in the house with me. But they first aks his mother. She say, "I ain't gonna tell no lie. This man is just as nice to us as he can be. We've been there on his place, and he never give me no trouble or anything. Whatever I aksed him to do, he did. My son, he's the fault of all of it. They tussled there on the bed and he hit him once or twice," she say. "But he ain't throwed no gun on him."

And Andrew Smith say, "Well, I charge you thirty dollars; you willin' to pay that?"

I say, "Not a penny!" I told him I wadn't willin' to pay a penny 'cause I hadn't done nothing. And we had another trial, and they turned me a'loose and I ain't had to pay a penny.

And they didn't bother me no more. But after then, Preacher Saffold and Link Williams—that's Cora's brother, he's dead now—we was about the onliest ones that stuck right through here. An' they didn't like us, but made like they like us. They don't bother us, treat just as nice; but still you can tell they got that hate in 'em. We had a hard time.

Once I went 'bout two miles from here where somebody had a goose, and a white guy—wasn't his place, but he was 'joining this white man's place. I drove up, and he was sittin' on the porch. And all beforehand he always nice to me—Roby this, Roby that. When I drove up, he look like he got mad. And I act like I didn't pay him no 'tention. So I told the lady why I'd come out there—my wife had said she had a goose. She say, "Yeah. Why don't y'all boys go out there and catch him?"

And look like he got so mad 'til he had to say something. He say, "Roby, you ain't wanted here. Got that white lady in your house."

I say, "What you got to do with this here? This ain't none of your place, is it? I'm tellin' you right now, that house belongs to me. I don't owe nobody nothin' on it. If I get a bunch of white-faced cows and put 'em in there, it's nobody's business. If I want to sleep with them, if I want 'em to stay with me, nobody have nothing to do with it. And that go for you and all the rest of 'em."

And so he went back and told them white folks that, and told me what they gonna do when they see me.

I say, "Well, I just wants to get it over with." I got up that morning, and I had a good gun. I let it lay there right there aside me. And I had a old pickup; I just put it in gear and let it roll on slow, and when I got near past the store, I was just driving along with my hand on it. And the three of 'em was sitting in the front of the store there. And nobody said a word. Nobody tried to stop me—nothing. I went on down to the foot of the hill and 'cross that bridge and turn around and came back that same way. And nobody said a word 'cause I was layin' for 'em. I may been the first one gone, but I was gonna carry somebody with me. And they ain't open their mouth from that day until this one.

CR: What kind of gun was it?

VR: Automatic pistol. Naw, I had my pump gun; not my pump gun but my rifle right under me. By law you have a right to carry a gun; just don't conceal it.

Did you march?

VR: Oh yes. Lord, we marched every time there come a march. We marched from Canton slam on into Jackson. We camped at Tougaloo campus after Martin Luther King made his speech. And they throwed that tear gas on us in Canton. I had never been in no tear gas before. Preacher sayin', "They gettin' ready to throw that gas; just lay down flat." But that didn't help none; that gas was [laughs] too tough. We had to get up from there and get away from it [laughs]. But, oh Lord, we went through something, I ain't joking with ya.

CR: One evening a white lady—a college student, I reckon, from Greenwood—came here to take a bath. She said there's a meeting out to the church. So we went on and she explained it—Head Start Program. She aksed who would be chairman of this program. Nobody said nothing. "Anybody thats willing to give it a try? Hold up your hand." So I begged Virgie [Saffold]. Again nobody said nothing. She held her hand up.

So they set the program up that night. But it was tough starting off; me and Virgie had a time. We had to wash and scrub and paint. Started with our kins and husbands; they would come with hammers and try and fix the place up. No food; we started off unorganized.

A lady gave us a old wood cooking stove, and they hired your great grandpa, Jodie, Sr., to come and get us a little wood and work the old stove to cook the children food. We would decide what we were gonna carry the next day. If I was gonna carry milk, meal, eggs, and butter, maybe she was gonna carry some flour, sugar. Then, finally, the government started sending supplies to the school.

Now at that time I was cooking and Virgie was teaching. We done the best we could. And they started paying me and paying Virgie, and they hired two cooks and I stopped cooking. And they hired an assistant for me and an assistant for Virgie. But we had a time at first.

What about the other blacks around here; they was just too scared to get involved?

VR: Well, yes.

CR: Some of 'em didn't have nothing to do with the Movement. . . .

VR: The preachers, number one, they didn't have nothing to do with it. Teachers, number two, they didn't have nothing to do with it. Until things got when they could tell that they wasn't gon' kill 'em, and then they went to comin' in.

CR: After jobs come in, they came in to get jobs.

VR: But now our chairman of the FDP, he was a hundred percent good. A little old preacher out there, Reverend Russell from Mileston; now he was good. He stuck with us. That's the onliest preacher I know's stayed with us.

CR: Now them other preachers, they knowed so many of their members was afraid, and they's afraid they wouldn't get no money. And the teachers were afraid they wouldn't get no jobs. The teachers didn't have anything to do with it.

VR: Bernice Montgomery, she stuck mighty well through this Movement. But the biggest of them had just turned back. Now Sue and Henry Lorenzi, they didn't have nothing but sense, and they had nerve, sho' 'nough. I hate it he dead now.

The time y'all first got involved, was any of y'all's kin trying to persuade you, "Look out, you fixin' to get yourself killed, and you wanna ease up a little bit"?

VR: I had some to say they was 'fraid we was gonna get killed. And I was lookin' for them to come through here and shoot. But I was layin' for 'em. Layin' in the bushes for 'em many a night. If they made a shot, I was intending to let 'em have it. But they never did it.

During that summer when those three civil rights workers, Chaney and Goodman and Schwerner, were killed down there in Philadelphia, that musta made you scared?

VR: Man, man, I'm tellin' you, I made up my mind to die, if I had to. It didn't make me no difference.

CR: I was afraid, I was afraid until I prayed. I was just trembling in my sleep. I say, "Well, Lord, I don't feel like I done done nothing wrong, 'cause these white peoples come for to try to help, and You must've sent 'em."

VR: Boy, but I'll tell you the truth. I'm still sticking in, doing the best I can till the good master call me. And intend to stay here. My brother-in-law, he passed and left. He stuck until the good master called him. T'was just a few of us. The Sisters, them white girls up at ROCC, now they still sticking with us, yeah. Some of 'em still comin' up standing, just a few—that's all.

Civil rights folks told us, "It ain't gonna be a lot of y'all, a few of you; but y'all stay. See, some of them got jobs and some of them get a little money in their pockets and get homes, and they slacken up," he say. "But y'all stay." And I'm still sticking the best I can.

MR. JODIE
"PREACHER" SAFFOLD

"I Caught Hell"

MARQUES SAFFOLD, JEFFREY BLACKMON,
& MARVIN NOEL

Mr. Jodie Saffold, Jr., commonly known as "Preacher," is a proud landowner. He was born in 1930 on a farm near West, Mississippi. He has two sisters and one brother; they all worked on the farm. When he was eighteen, he went into the Army; and when he came out, he bought himself one hundred eighty-two acres of land for sixteen hundred dollars cash. He believes land makes black men powerful, and he was very active in the Civil Rights Movement. Mr. Saffold is the father of three intelligent girls. If you meet Preacher, you will never forget him.

Preacher's wife, Mrs. Virgie Saffold, was also a civil rights activist. She traveled to South Carolina, where she attended a citizenship training workshop taught by Septima Clark, Andrew Young, and Dorothy Cotton of the Southern Christian Leadership Conference (SCLC). When she came back, she had the know-how to teach people in her community what she had learned. Virgie Saffold has been the head teacher at the Old Pilgrim Rest's Head Start center for twenty-five years. Right along side Preacher, she was a strong Movement supporter from the beginning. Preacher always carried a pistol for protection, but when things got rough he was worried that the police would search him and find the pistol. So Virgie took the gun and carried it in her purse when they went to town, and Preacher seldom left her side.

Mr. Saffold was injured by heavy machinery on a pulpwood yard back in the '70s, and he has been limping ever since. But he still works in the field and around the house. He has cows, horses, pigs, and seven dogs. He doesn't do work like younger folks; they work and stop and start back again. No, he goes ahead and gets his work done. He likes playing games, but when it's time to work, he means business.

Mr. Jodie is my grand-daddy. He taught me to go ahead and do what older people tell you and not to be slowing around. He is a very strict teaching person (if you do wrong, you will get whipped), but he is also very warm-hearted. I stayed with him for about eight or nine years, but as I got older, I got bored because there wasn't anyone to play with at his home, way out in the country. So I left, but I still go back every once in a while. We interviewed Preacher at his farm, near Old Pilgrim Rest.

—MARQUES SAFFOLD

[In the following interview, **JS** is Mr. Jodie Saffold, Jr.]

Tell me a little bit about the Civil Rights Movement.

JS: What you want me to tell, Marques?

Mr. Saffold, who was the first people involved in the Civil Rights Movement?

JS: I would say Norman Clark, Ralthus Hayes, T. C. Johnson, and, in this area, me and Link Williams and Vanderbilt Roby, my cousins. It was the so-called dumb people. Up from the grassroots, they call it. But now, the school teachers, the educated people, they ain't did a damn thang! The preachers ain't neither. The so-called dumb people open the way for everybody. See, the table was set. Yeah, and when the table got set with cake and pie, school teachers and everybody come in helping eat it up.

And they were the ones that was mostly elected?

JS: Yeah.

And most of the people, the farmers and the so-called uneducated, was the ones that spent the blood, sweat, and tears to get everyone registered to make that possible?

JS: The folks in office ain't done a damn thang. I'll stand up on a block anywhere and tell 'em. Poor T. C. Johnson did ever'thang; then they won't let 'em have no office, and I think it's wrong. I don't feel good about it.

Mr. Saffold, I heard that the Civil Rights Movement didn't form from Rosa Parks but started from Emmett Till? Is that true?

JS: Mmm, it didn't start from Emmett Till. It really started in '64, but Emmett Till was lynched. They didn't do much about that; they did nothing to them people.

Do you remember anything about Emmett Till?

JS: Mmm, yeah, I remember it, but I just couldn't get any low downs on it. He made a lust; he made a whistle at a white girl. And they kill him and put weight around his neck and threw him in the river. You know that was the end. They didn't do nothing to them honkies when

Emmett Till was lynched. He just was a dead black man. Wasn't no Movement then. He was down on a vacation and this happened.

What was your reaction when he died?

JS: What was my reaction? Well, I really didn't have a reaction because we didn't have no Movement then; and whatever the white man said, the white man was the law. He made the law and broke it. The black people didn't have too much power then, when they lynched Emmett Till.

Could you borrow something from the bank? You know, when blacks was fired from their jobs, they couldn't get no loans; farmers couldn't get no loans.

JS: Well, the laws kind of got properly. . . . You can get all the money you want after the Movement. See, the main thing is power. You take back into the '60s. If I hadn't had land, I couldn't took those civil rights workers in my home. The white man found out, right shortly after '64, that all the power was in the landowners, and then they went to buying it up. And damn near all the blacks sold a lot of their land. See, the honky knowed where the power was; then they went to buying up land. See, right now y'all seating here, I can tell y'all to get away; I can make you move from here. Then, the black people didn't have sense enough to know that their land was still one of the powerful things they have in the world.

Did your grandfather teach you that?

JS: Well, yeah, my grandfather taught me that, and my cousin Benny Montgomery. Yes, they believe in land. They believe in land.

The real strength of the Movement came from the farmers that own their own land. . . . Could you tell me, if you had got your home taken, how you would have felt?

JS: I paid for my home cash. It has never been under mortgage.

Was it anyone else they did that way? Did you have any friends, with their house mortgaged, that they tried to mess with and discourage?

JS: They gave them a hard time, but I really didn't know anyone who just lost their home.

Now, you take where I was borrowin' money at, as I put Cleveen in the white school. See, I was doing business through GCA, which is the Greenwood Credit Association. I went in to pay. When I walked in the place, the white guy, he said to me, "Jodie, where your kids go to school at?"

I said, "Down by the fire department."

He said, "Where?"

I said, "In the white school!"

When I said that, he said, "You can get on out of here."

That was in Lexington?

JS: Yeah.

What did you do then?

JS: I walked right outta there. My wife had a dime and called headquarters in Greenwood and told how he had did us. You know, I had sense enough to know he was working there for the salary, and I knew it wasn't none of his money.

Do you think the people in Greenwood wanted to fire him?

JS: Well, I told a couple of civil rights workers. I wouldn't really say they did it, but finally he kinda quit work there. He got fired, I think. I wouldn't say they fired him; but shortly after then, I got a letter from the headquarters, and they told me where to go, and I had another representative by the name of D. C. Scott—he was the head dude here in Lexington. And that's who I did business with. Got where I could do my own thing.

You didn't have any more problems after this?

JS: Unh! Unh! Unh! Unh! With the school integration, *again*. Cleveen, she was kind of shy to go, and I kept beggin' her, telling her what I would do for her if she go. I told her I was goin' to give all the money she wanted for pretty clothes. I wanted her to better her condition. And so I finally got her to say she would go, and I carried her down and enrolled her. It wasn't nothin' there but mostly whites, and I didn't sit right beside her. And I kinda slightly looked back at Veen, and she was just cryin'. Tears was just droppin'. She didn't want to be there with all them white kids, and then I cried too—but she didn't know.

She had been at school a couple of days. So we out there pickin' cotton that evening and Veen got off the bus, and she come out there runnin'. She says, "Daddy, this is a letter from the teacher." And my wife got the letter and read it, and she said for one of the parents come— mother or daddy. And my wife said to me, "You are the man, you go. Get clean." So I put on the best suit I had. So I goes down there to the white school. Teacher ask me, "You Jodie Saffold?"

"Yeah." I said. "What do you want?"

She say, "Your child, she don't wanna be here. Don't you see her sittin' over there by herself? She ain't playing and she ain't happy like the other kids."

I say, "Well Missus, the little schooling I got, I didn't know you suppose to play in the classroom. I thought when you was in the classroom you suppose to be down there working."

She said, "If you would take her out, the thirty dollars you paid for workbooks, you can get it back."

I said, "Naw, I ain't gon' take her out." So I come on back home and she didn't have no more trouble. And then she went on, she went on to school.

Couple weeks later, she says, "Daddy, they done pull all the whites out now." And this civil rights worker, girl by the name of Donna Lopez, she was teaching down here. So when she came in that evening, we told her that. She say, "Well I'm goin' to integrate it." So she left that night in her car and drove to Jackson and flew back to New York. She had a little white girl; she flew her back in here and fixed her up a birth certificate, and she put her in the school.

She stay right there in the house. Everyday, she will be right there playing with my kids, and the whites would be passing by. Now, far as talking about the Movement, I caught hell. I got threats, you know.

Any volunteers stay with you?

JS: When the three civil rights workers got assassinated in Philadelphia, I kept workers, about two or three here. And Lopez, she stayed here about a year.

And did they catch any hard times?

JS: Well, not too much, 'though *they* didn't like it. But one of them went out here to West, trying to get people ready to vote. And the supervisor what we got now, Doug Green, run 'em away from his house. And there was another guy, I believe he was from New York; he was by the name of Zack. And he went down to a lil' store out there in West. And this here honky kicked him. They caught a lil' hell, but me and Vanderbilt and Link Williams is the ones that caught the hell and got the threats. But, in this community, in Pilgrim Rest community, we was the only three that took 'em.

What else did they try to do to discourage you from being active in the Movement?

JS: I got a lot of threats. Late every Saturday evening, you see a load of white people; they would drive by my house, right slow, and they would go down to the turn of the road and come back driving real slow, just lookin', you know. That was to scare me. And then, they were watchin' me.

So one evenin', I had been carryin' a gun 'cause I said, if they were gon' kill me, I was gon' try to get me some. We was comin' on back from carryin' a neighbor, Ella, home. And so I seed this honky boy on the tractor, and the tractor was goin' loud so he didn't know I was behind him. So I tooted my horn and it scared him, so he darted out the road. So I passed on by, and I carried Ella and put Ella out. Then when I got back there, this white boy was settin' on the tractor, and his daddy parked double in the road and had the road block on me. And I drove on up and he said, "Jimmy say you was meddlin' with him."

"No, I wasn't meddlin' with Jimmy; I was carryin' my neighbor home." And he pull out the gun and put it in my face. I wasn't scared, but I had sense enough to know, if he pull the trigger, it would kill me. So, I turn around and went on home the other way.

They threaten us, but we didn't really care 'cause we were ready to die. I still feel that way. I don't mind dying 'cause the cause good. We didn't really care.

Do you know of any freedom schools around here?

JS: Yeah, they had one here. The volunteers that was living here, Bob and Dave. Every day, they would go up to the church. That's what they was here for. Yeah, they had freedom schools.

Right at the Old Pilgrim Rest?

JS: Yeah, they had freedom school every day for six weeks.

Did you ever know what they was teaching?

JS: Well, they were teaching how to register and vote. We didn't know anything about that. A honky didn't want you to vote; white people didn't want you to vote in Mississippi.

Did you have any children to go?

JS: Yeah, they would go.

Did you have to pay poll taxes?

JS: Yeah, we paid taxes a few times. They didn't want that to happen. They didn't want a black to pay poll taxes. Me, Link, Vanderbilt, and Daddy paid poll tax a couple of times.

When did you first try to register to vote?

JS: Well, about the last part of '63 or '64. We come to register to vote; they had that literacy [test] so hard for the blacks. And my wife, she went to a farm on South Carolina with the school. She go over there and stay 'bout a week. Then she'd come back here, and she would have class with this black freedom school. Then she would go from community to community. Like on Friday nights she'd have class, teaching 'em how to register and vote. She'd go back over there once every month to the workshop.

Do you remember if the Klan ever burned crosses?

JS: They didn't burn down here, but I think they burned one at Uncle Link's house.

When Freedom Summer came, were you happy or something? How did you feel?

JS: You know I was happy. I wanted to come out from under slavery. Yeah, I was happy. Yeah, I was very happy. I put my life on the line; I marched; I done every damn thing. You know I was happy; I was over-rejoiced. I didn't want to come like my grand-daddy come. And I didn't want my kids to come like I did. Yeah, I was happy; I did every thang I could, I pull ever' string I knowed.

What happened in the Canton parade? How far did y'z.'l have to march?

JS: Marched in Benton and I marched from Benton to Canton. We got into Canton that evening about five o'clock. Then we went down there to this old school. When we got there, we seen all the patrollers standing around; had us surrounded. And then Dr. King's comin' there, and he get there on the platform. He made a big speech, and he told that they don't want us to pitch the tent; but we gon' pitch the tent. So when they start puttin' the tent up, they put the gas mask on.

Then they went to sprayin' tear gas. People started runnin' and then my father was standin' right next to me. When I seed 'em get them masks I knew what they gon' do, 'cause I was familiar with that tear gas when I was in the service. So, I told my daddy, I said, "They fixin' to gas us!" And, I told him to get his hancher [handkerchief] and tie it o'er your face. Then everybody started runnin' and we scattered.

And we come home after they gassed us. And then that Sunday, they had made it to Tougaloo, so we went to Jackson, come back to Tougaloo that Sunday. So we marched from Tougaloo on into Jackson, and we made it there about four or five o'clock that Sunday evening; so everything was cool.

They say the Movement was nonviolent, but in Mississippi it seemed like most people had guns to defend themselves.

JS: Well, yeah, Dr. King wanted to see nonviolent; if they slap you on the jaw, turn the other cheek. But if they hit, I was gon' hit 'em back.

Is that the way most folks felt in Mississippi?

JS: Yeah, some of 'em.

Was there disagreements about that ever?

JS: It was nonviolent, but I was gon' hit back. I was gon' hit back. You know, it wasn't but three of us, and Vanderbilt said he was gon' fight back and Link said he was gon' fight back, and I told 'em I damn sure was gon' fight back. We didn't have no help, not in this community.

After World War II, there was lots of people that been to war, blacks that had been to war and had been segregated. But they saw they could die for their country and everything else, and they come back to Mississippi. They were some of the ones that had been involved in the Movement, too. They were a lot less willing to be treated like second-class citizens, like a DOG. *A honky will treat you like a dog.*

MRS. BERNICE MONTGOMERY JOHNSON

Teacher of the Movement

KENNETH SALLIS & TAMARA WRIGHT

The reason we decided to interview Mrs. Johnson was that other people we interviewed mentioned that she was the only schoolteacher from Holmes County who participated in the Civil Rights Movement. We felt that our book would not be complete without her story. We have tremendous respect for Mrs. Johnson because of her involvement in the Movement at a time when other teachers refrained from participating.

Mrs. Johnson is a short, heavily built elderly woman. Her complexion is very light-skinned, and she wears glasses. She speaks her mind and is very serious about what she does. She is well educated and articulates her words carefully.

Mrs. Johnson started out in the Movement by simply opening up her home to civil rights workers. Eventually she also became involved in activities such as encouraging people to register to vote and to hold meetings in their community. She told us that she was not afraid to get involved in the Movement initially, because she did not have an understanding of the real dangers that were out there. Later on, however, she did become afraid privately; nobody else ever knew about her fear.

Mrs. Johnson's chldren were among those who integrated the white school in Lexington in 1965 and subsequent years. In 1967, after she had taught in the Holmes County school system for twenty-three years, Mrs. Johnson was asked to direct the Head Start program and she accepted.

Mrs. Johnson is now living in Jackson, Mississippi, where she runs a home for elderly people. But her roots are in Holmes County, and she often comes back to visit.

[In the following interview, **BJ** is Mrs. Bernice Montgomery Johnson.]

Mrs. Johnson, how did you get involved in the Civil Rights Movement?

BJ: I guess it was in the early '60s when there were quite a few civil rights workers that came into Mississippi, and they were needing a place to live at that time. And, of course, I opened my doors for them to come and make themselves at home and do whatever work they were going to do with the people in the community. In talking with them every night when I came home from work, I found their concerns to be of interest to me. And I simply joined in and started to do whatever I could to educate our community.

Why weren't you afraid to become involved in the beginning?

BJ: I guess it was the lack of an understanding what the consequences could be. I never thought about bombings and killings and lynchings. I was just so excited and motivated to the point that I wanted to help educate our people so we could enjoy some liberties. It was maybe a year or two later, after I saw things really happen in the state of Mississippi, that I got somewhat afraid. Because I witnessed a lot of unpleasant things, and I found out that it could be dangerous—for me and my family—to be involved in activities such as these. There were other families where there was a tragedy—you know, shootings, bombings into houses, especially like that of Mr. Turnbow. It could've happened to me. Because I was keeping white people in my house the same as he was. I didn't express it. Nobody knew that I was afraid, but I was.

Why was it that you were the only teacher involved in the Movement?

BJ: Well, there were quite a few threats in the county; people saying if teachers became involved in anything like this, you gonna lose your job or you gonna get killed. So naturally teachers were afraid. They didn't even want to be seen talking to me, because they thought I might be saying something that would encourage them to become involved in the Movement.

Did anybody else get involved, try to back you up?

BJ: We were with the grassroots people, the local people out in the community at Old Pilgrim Rest, at Sunny Mount and Mileston. Really all the Movement started in Mileston. And my husband and I were the first people from the hills to go down in the Delta to Mileston and join the Movement.

Later on we encouraged other people to go. But if professional people were really afraid of losing their job, of losing what they had, they didn't want to participate. Because now when you talk about fear, they were *really* afraid to become involved. But it never dawned on me at first. For some reason, it was kind of funny to me when I would be going along the road, watching the highway patrolman trailing me off to the side of the road, watching me go by. And I'd just laugh and keep going; say, "There he is over there!" I was not engulfed in fear at that time. When we first started, my husband and I were going to Mileston, to a little old church down across the railroad track from the Mileston store—that's where the meetings originated.

How exactly did the Movement spread from Mileston throughout the whole county?

BJ: Well, they were constantly trying to get new members. I remember when I first started going to Mileston, I encouraged the people in the community where I lived (which was Sunny Mount) to start having a meeting. And Old Pilgrim Rest became involved at about the same time. We were constantly going from community to community, from church to church, asking people to allow us to come into your church: "Would you become involved? Set you up a community meeting. Elect you some officers—a president, a secretary, a treasurer or what have you—and designate a certain time for your community meetings.

We heard of only one preacher being involved in the Movement here and that was Reverend Russell. Why was it that other preachers just weren't really involved in the Movement here in Holmes County?

BJ: It was because of fear. There was any number of churches that were burned if they even allowed us to come in and have a meeting. Ministers and church officials were afraid to let us come in, afraid they were going to be bombed, that they'd lose their church. It wasn't 'til later years that we got other ministers involved. But Reverend Russell was the very first one.

See, people were afraid; people were constantly telling me I'd be killed. They even convinced my mother and father to talk me out of that mess, as they called it, and my mother and father were constantly saying, "You're gonna get killed. Your house is gonna be bombed, you're gonna lose your little children. You need to stop; you don't need to do this." So there was somebody out there constantly frightening people, because we was trying to get the right to vote. And with Holmes County being predominantly black—it was 73 percent blacks at that time—Holmes County black people could elect anybody they wanted to. Then we would have control of Holmes County. So the other race did not want to see that happen. So they would pry on weaker people—to try to get through to us, to say that something was gonna happen to you if you don't stop.

Exactly what was your role in the Movement?

BJ: For years I was secretary of the county-wide Movement; even before there was an FDP I served as secretary for all the county-wide meetings.

I helped teach voter education, and I worked for voter registration, helped to organize selective buying campaigns, marches. I served on a biracial committee for getting problems solved in Holmes County. Any number of things. I worked day and night.

Were most of these committees you served on effective?

BJ: When you look at Holmes County today, you would say they were effective. Because we achieved some of the goals we set out to do: You've got a black sheriff, black Board of Supervisors, a black tax assessor, and all those things. You know, not too long ago I was just riding along, thinking about all the offices that were lily-white. They were controlled by whites, whites, whites. No black person was seen in an office doing anything. That small percentage of whites controlled Holmes County. But it's not true today, so what we were doing then was effective. It took time, but you can see the results today.

What ran through people's minds when you went to their house asking them to register to vote? How did they react?

BJ: At first it was not a house-to-house campaign. Holmes County is divided into beats, and we divided it into precincts; then the precincts were divided into communities. And in every community there was a major church. And we chose that major church as a meeting place, once we convinced people that nothing was gonna happen to them.

Every community had a certain meeting night. And we, at the county level, would go to that place, and that's where we would start teaching them what the effects would be once they became registered voters. They had to learn what beat they lived in: Where is my voting precinct, where do I go to vote, what am I s'posed to do when I get there, what will I be looking for . . . ? They had to learn all those things before they were actually ready to go to the polls and let somebody scare them to death. See, there were people that went to the polls and there someone would say: "Boy, what you come here for? You wanna buy a mule?" Just things like that. And then some of them would get afraid and wouldn't go back. But we would do mock elections. I had all the fun I wanted doing mock elections. Because I would [laughs] play the role of an election official and would have people come in, and I would say, "Boy, what did you come in here for?"

"I want to register to vote."

"Well, what you wanna vote for? You wanna know how many potatoes you gonna dig this year?"

I would just say something to throw them off, to let them understand: "Now, when you go, you might hear this. I'm just playing with you now, but when you go up to register, you might hear something even sillier than this. But be firm and say: 'I came to register to vote.' "

Now first you had to fill out that four-page questionnaire and interpret the section of the Constitution. But what we would tell them is, "Go try it anyway so we can prove they did this to you. But it's not legal. You're supposed to be able to register to vote, because you're a citizen of this county. But they're gonna tell you you can't, because you can't pass this questionnaire."

And I would always try to be the example. Whatever came up, I'll go. If we had to go to court for something, I'll be the plaintiff. I'll go, and let's just see what would happen to me. So during the Christmas holidays of 1963, I convinced two other teachers to go with me: Let's fill out this questionnaire so that all people know nothing happened to us. We'll be the example. So we went in around Christmas, about the 20th of December. And they treated us so bad: "Come in here, girl! What you coming for? Sit over here, you not gonna stay in the same room. One of you over here, and one over there." And they talked to us so rough and so cruel. I could look around and see them just trembling down. I was trembling too, because it was just frightening the way they talked to us. They separated us and put us in a little dingy room to fill out this questionnaire. I filled mine out, and I interpreted the section of the Constitution that they told me to. They said, "Well, you won't know today. You have to come back in thirty days to find out if you passed this test." So I went back in the latter part of January of '64. And the circuit clerk said, "Well, you passed the test, but you ain't gonna become no registered voter because you didn't put down the right beat."

I said, "Yes, I did." And the courthouse was just filled with white peoples standing all around, seeing what was gonna happen. And I know it was embarrassing to him when I said, "You know, and everybody else in here knows, that I put down the right beat. Because we're neighbors. I live on one side the beat line, which is Beat One; you live on the other side, which is Beat Two. You know where I live. I know where you live. I'm in Beat One."

"You live in Beat Two."

I said, "Oh no, I don't live in Beat Two. You live in Beat Two. But the line divides us."

See, we has studied these beat lines, precinct lines, and community dividing lines. We knew them; we had taught them to everybody in Holmes County, community by community. So finally, he turned real red and said: "Well, come on round here and sign the book." So I went round and signed the book. And to my knowledge, I am the first black person in Holmes County that became a registered voter at that time. Now some years before that, there was a group of teachers at Ambrose High, I think, went in and registered. And when the white people found out they had registered, they made them go back and take their names off the rolls: "If you don't, you are fired. You won't have a job, and you stand a chance of getting your house bombed." Now those people were more afraid than anybody else in the county.

Why did they want to get their names off the rolls?

BJ: Because black people were not allowed to vote. They were not allowed to register to vote. So they had to take their names off. And it was in later years, after this questionnaire was outlawed, that they came back and registered again. But they actually went back and scratched their names off the rolls.

Now the other two ladies who went to register with me—I don't know to this day if they went back to see if they passed. I think they were so afraid of that abuse. I have talked to one of them in particular since: "What day did you go back?" And she has not answered me. So I really think they waited 'til this old test had been outlawed and then went and registered.

On the days it was time to vote, what was the reaction of some of the local whites up there?

BJ: On election days it appeared that everybody would be upset; people would be standing around watching—black people and white, too—to see who was going in that courthouse. As if the sight of white people was gonna frighten you. . . . I never had the occasion of having any white people do anything or say anything to me at that time. I guess when they found out I was really concerned about what I was doing, there was no turning back. I was gonna do this no matter what anybody said; I didn't have the harassment that a lot of people had. So what they thought about me, I don't know. They would stare and look, and that's about the height of what they did so far as me being involved and my activities.

What was the cause of them bombing Hartman Turnbow's house?

BJ: Well, you see, when the out-of-state civil rights workers came in, Mr. Turnbow was housing two white nurses, because there was a little clinic set up down in Mileston, and that's where they lived. He had been warned to get those white people out of his house, because blacks and whites did not live together in Holmes County, Mississippi. And they had threatened him with what they would do if he didn't get them out. He simply said: "This is my house and I invite anybody I want to come in, no matter what their color is." So they were holding that against him—having his house integrated—as much as they were trying to prohibit him from becoming a registered voter.

What organizations were involved in the Movement?

BJ: The Freedom Democratic Party was the major organization in the county. We had community- and county-level FDPs. And, of course, there was COFO and SNCC that came into the county from other places. But Holmes Countians were involved in FDP.

Exactly what was the FDP?

BJ: The Freedom Democratic Party was a state-wide organization. But it was broken down county by county. And this organization dealt primarily with community problems, voter registration, voter education, community involvement.

Were there any citizenship classes?

BJ: Yes, there were weekly meetings that were held from church to church. There were citizenship classes. But they were broken down into a lot of areas.

Were you involved in school integration?

BJ: Yes. The first grade was integrated first in Holmes County. And my baby was first grade that year. That was a nervous moment, but I was determined to go through with it. I think I had more problems getting her enrolled in school than all the other families put together. I took my baby down and they said: "You don't have a certified birth certificate, and so we can't let her enter the first grade."

And there was a white attorney here living with me at this time—Mel Leventhal. I said, "Mel, they said they weren't going to let Evita enroll, because her birth certificate is not certified."

Now while Mel was around there at the school, usually he'd be dressed up all in his suit and his tie on. He said, "Get in the car. Let's go to Jackson." He would pull that tie off, and get his coat off so fast, and I don't know why the highway patrol didn't pick us up because sometimes he'd be driving eighty, ninety miles an hour from Lexington to Jackson. We went down there to the Bureau of Birth Certificates and got another certificate.

They wouldn't take that one. And they told us, "It's no need of you going to Jackson again, because if she doesn't have the birth certificate by four o'clock today, she's not going to be able to enroll." We took off to Jackson again and got another birth certificate and got back to Lexington at ten minutes to four, and we go in and got her reigistered.

Now the other fellows had the same kind of birth certificate as Evita originally had, but they figured that if they could make me go sit down and hush, they could conquer a lot of other people. They were determined not to let my child register.

Well, the next year, the whole school was integrated. I'm the mother of nine children, and three of my children had already graduated from high school. So I had six children went into the integrated system. And for three years straight, the only black child that graduated from the old so-called white school was my child. Byron was the first one, and he graduated with honors. Next was Wilamena. Things happened that were really kind of comical. When I would go to parents' night or whatever, even to the graduation exercise, I would always get there early. I'd sit down, and when they dismissed, I would be the only person sitting on the row, because white parents would come in and started down there, and they'd look up, see me, and whirl around and get another seat. So I was the only black parent in there and the only person sitting on this long row of seats.

Now that happened for three years straight, 'til my third child graduated from high school. And that's when all the white children pulled out and left nothing but black children. So that's when that school became the Lexington Elementary School.

Why did you involve your children in school integration?

BJ: I think the white school was better. And my children can witness this: Black schools did not get the books nor equipment that the white schools got. When the white children wore out their books, they got brand-new books and gave the old ragged books to the black children. That lab right over there at the former Lexington Attendance Center hardly had a test-tube in it. But the white schools were well equipped. And I wanted my children to really get the best education. And I wanted all children to know that they had a right to a good education. Let my children be an example, having the opportunity to use some of these things that was theirs. Those things were put in those white schools by black tax-paying money. The county was predominantly black, so that was black tax money going into that school. So why shouldn't my children enjoy some of it? I think my children's achievements were great because of that.

But did you ever fear for your children?

BJ: Now the oldest boy that went there was my fourth child. He was big and stocky, and he was an A-student. Nobody ever bothered him about anything. And so I didn't have any fear for Byron. The next one was Wilamena; she wasn't all that big, but she was kind of pushy, herself. She could handle herself with anybody in the classroom, with her teachers and anybody else. And she was very vocal about what she was doing and what she wanted to do. The next one was Myzell; he wasn't quite so big and stocky; he wasn't quite so vocal. He was a good student but quiet. And one day somebody called me: "You'd better go on out to the school, because Myzell has been in a fight!"

I said, "Not Myzell, the quietest child I have."

"Yes, he's been in a fight."

I said, "Oh, Lord they been waiting for a reason to kick him out of school. So now he's gonna be expelled." And I ran to the school, to the principal's office. He said, "Mrs. Montgomery, what can I do for you?"

I said, "I heard Myzell was in a fight."

He said, "How did you hear that? We had planned not to even worry you about it, because this white boy has been meddlin' Myzell for weeks. We knew it, and we have talked to him about it. Today he got out of line, crossed over right in front of Myzell, and hit Myzell with his elbow. Myzell laid his books down, threw him down in the hall, and gave him a good beating. Myzell came into the office," he said, "and talked to me just like a little man. He said, 'I didn't come over here to get in trouble. I didn't come over here to be involved in a fight. I want the best education possible, because I want to make something out of myself. And I don't want any teacher to think I came over here to cause trouble, because I didn't,' he said. 'But I had taken this for about three weeks and I couldn't take it anymore. And before I knew it, I had grabbed him and downed him on the floor.' " So the principal said, "I sat there and listened to him. And I was proud of the way he expressed himself. So you didn't have anything to worry about." And I thought he was a great principal.

But that's the only time I had a little fear: While I was driving over there, I was thinking all kinds of thoughts. But everything was positive; nothing really happened.

Do you know the numbers of blacks that enrolled in this school?

BJ: I would say it wasn't more than twelve in the first grade. When the entire school was integrated, I would say about fifteen or twenty.

When you all integrated the schools, were there any lawyers involved?

BJ: Yes. I mentioned Mel Leventhal, who was an attorney that was here. There was him, Lawrence Guyot, and quite a few lawyers. We would sit up sometimes all night listening to them explaining to us what our rights were, what's the best way to do this, how to express yourself, and those kinds of things.

In what year did the whites start leaving the school after blacks came in?

BJ: It must have been '68 or '69. Because I think Byron graduated in '68. That's what I'm going by. There were private schools set up all over the county—academies. And they went into these academies. They had private funding. And they paid tuition to go to high school. But I understand that they don't have to worry too much about tuition. Because they get plenty of private funding—foundations or what have you.

What were some of the outcomes of school integration?

BJ: Afterwards, even though the whites had pulled out, there was more support from the State Department of Education for black schools when it comes to buildings and equipment and everything else, since they had only black schools. That's one positive angle that you can think of.

Well, how did Head Start put an effect on the Movement?

BJ: Head Start was designed to meet the needs of the preschool child and his or her family and the community. Now, when you're speaking in terms of family and community, that took in everything that was going on in the community. And that is why Head Start was labeled as something bad that came into the county, and a lot of whites didn't want it. Now when I was hired as a director of the first Head Start program that came in, I was in the school system. I had taught twenty-three years. That was in '67.

The first month we got our checks, wouldn't a bank in Lexington cash them. Hundreds of people had checks because they had worked, but not a bank would cash a Head Start check. Because it was the name of something bad: "We don't want it in here. They are going to ruin all the black peoples in the county. They are teaching them things they shouldn't be doing." But all we were trying to do is to teach them how to be good citizens and live at home and at peace with everybody. But they didn't want to see that. There was one white man—and I'll give him credit—Mr. King, who had the Five and Ten Cents store at that time, and he said, "Bernice, this is ridiculous. I tell you what you do: Bring the checks to me and I am going to deposit them to my store account, and I'll let your people have that money through my account." He's old and retired now, but that's the only way we could get our checks cashed.

Later on, when we were funded for the Holmes County Research program, I was still director of the Head Start program; and I was chosen at the same time to be the principal investigator for the Research program. And we brought in three-quarters of a million dollars a year. But now these banks wanted this money. I couldn't believe these were the same people. All the banks in the county wanted us: "Are you gonna bank with us? Are you gonna put this money in my bank?"

When I went to the bank to start negotiating for our accounts, they pulled out the chair for me: "Would you like to sit here?" I was knocked off my feet, they were so nice. But we decided to bank—especially in this Lexington and Delta area—to bank with all of them. We put Head Start money in one bank, and Research money in another bank. We even put some money for our special account down to Tchula. So we spreaded it around; tried to be as democratic as we possibly could.

Head Start really gave community people an insight as to what life is supposed to be. We educated the entire community through Head Start and the Research program. That was the best research program that I know of right now. We did a complete census of Holmes County. We divided the county up—by beats, by precincts, by communities— and we assigned so many people to every community that reported back to the precinct. Then the precinct reported back to the beats, and the beats reported to the central county level. And we charted every house in Holmes County on a map—whether someone was living in it or whether it was empty. And we had somebody to go to every house personally and count the people in that house. We were naturally concerned about preschool children, and we found children who were nine and ten years old—black and white—that had never been to school a day in their lives. But we found them back in the boondogs and the woods, just back there. I remember we found one little white boy that had never been to school, and he was ten years old. "Well, he doesn't have any clothes." We went and bought him clothes. Mrs. Marie Moore was social services director for Head Start, and that was her goal—to find every child and see to it that he got the kind of services he needed. So we took him and sent him to a Head Start center along with some three or four year olds, and at the end of that month he was ready to enter the first grade. He wasn't the only one—just one I thought of right then. So Head Start played a vital role for that child, his family, and the community.

Were you ever part of Community Action Program (CAP)?

BJ: Yes. Head Start program was what you call the delegate agency. The federal government set it up that all money coming into this area had to go through the CAP agency over this district, and we had to get our funding through CAP—the Community Action agency. The central office was in Winona. The CAP director was I. P. Presley.

So who controlled all the money? The CAP?

BJ: It was controlled by the community. The CAP agency covered several counties and so many people from all those counties. There were Holmes, Attala, Choctaw, Montgomery, and Carroll. Those counties made up this CAP area, and so many representatives from each county made up the CAP Board. And the CAP Board controlled the monies.

What was the number of blacks on this Board?

BJ: Oh, the Board was predominantly black, but there was a sizable number of whites.

The whites didn't try to take over?

Ozell Mitchell, photographed on his Mileston farm in 1968. He and his sister, Alma Mitchell Carnegie, were two of the grassroots people who began the Holmes County Movement in early spring 1963. Apart from Bernice Montgomery Johnson, middle-class blacks in the county shunned the Movement during the dangerous early years.

BJ: Well, I don't think they could have. Because at that point in time, people had learned that I've got as much right as you have. And nobody's going to take over. We even had black people who were controversial on the CAP Board. And sometimes community people would have to kind of get the black CAP Board members in line. Because you always have black folks that want to cater to white folks.

How did this organization really help Holmes County?

BJ: It served as an entity to channel money through. But from my perspective, I could have done a much better job directing the program that I was directing without that CAP agency, because they was so far behind. See, the director of that CAP agency had never participated in any Movement activities, didn't really know what was going on; and— believe it or not—you can have teachers in a classroom with Ph.D.s who are ill-informed. They don't know what's going on outside those four walls in that classroom. They don't really know anything about the beat system in the county and elections and stuff. And they were afraid to find out. So you had a lot of teachers that came out of the classroom saying, "I want to work with this CAP agency," but they knew nothing about community involvement, what the needs of the people are, because they always thought they were so high-minded; they didn't want to come down there to these people in the Movement. And that's who controlled the Movement—the grassroots people. There was a lot of our own black people that looked down their nose at other folks. See, once upon a time the only professional job in Holmes County was a schoolteacher. And that's really the only thing now—a schoolteacher. So they thought they were better than everybody else. I was a teacher, but I felt that if this person is down on the ground, I can't get up or do anything until he gets up. Those people did not become registered voters until these people down here got up and paved the way for them to go ahead. They didn't do it—the little people did. And I give credit to the grassroots people for whatever was done in Holmes County.

MRS. VIOLA WINTERS

"Struggling 'Til God Call Me"

TAMARA WRIGHT & MICHAEL HOOKER

We liked Mrs. Viola Winters from the moment we walked into her house because she treated us like adults; she didn't talk down to us. Mrs. Winters has a small face and little gray eyes. On the day of the interview, she wore a beautiful bright dress of rainbow colors. Mrs. Winters is a widow who had eight children until one died. Every last one of her children is living up North. Her own father died when she was nine years old. She went to school in Gages Spring, but that school went only up to the eighth grade.

Framed pictures of her family dot her walls and bookshelves. She has a huge painting of Dr. Martin Luther King, Malcolm X, and a little boy crying, with Jesus Christ on the cross in the background. That painting made us remember how many people gave their lives so that we might be free. Mrs. Viola Winter's idol was Mrs. Fannie Lou Hamer. Like Mrs. Hamer, Mrs. Winters is energetic and fiery.

During the Movement, Mrs. Winters did so much for Durant and Holmes County. After registering to vote, she helped others register at the courthouse in Lexington. Her children had finished school, but she supported the first black children who tried to integrate the schools. She helped integrate the ice cream parlor, the railroad station, and the Durant Hospital. She also helped force the hospital to quit making people pay a fifty-dollar deposit before they could be admitted. She fought for jobs in the factories and went to Washington, D.C., when blacks were not hired as promised. Mrs. Winters participated in marches and took freedom riders into her home. She was a strong supporter of the Freedom Democratic Party and still attends its weekly meetings in Durant. Today she still struggles for what she struggled for in the '60s: liberty and justice for all.

[In the following interview, **VW** is Mrs. Viola Winters.]

☙

First of all, Mrs. Winters, I would like to ask you what got you interested in the Civil Rights Movement?

VW: After some of the civil rights workers come here from up North, I just got interested in it after I knowed it was all about integrating and justice. And I been following it ever since. When we went out in '64, we went out to integrate. We wanted justice and equal rights. We didn't wanna have a side door for the colored and one for the whites.

Did y'all have meetings beforehand to plan what you were going to do?

VW: Oh yes. We went to having meetings in the homes. They wouldn't let me have it in my house; white people was living here then. I told 'em I wasn't afraid; have it if they want to, but they didn't. Lotta them was afraid. Mildred Hills and her sister was the only ones that would let 'em have the meeting in their home. We met out there to plan at Second Pilgrim Rest Church with the Freedom Democratic Party—the FDP.

When we first started, we had the civil rights workers. They were white and colored, come here from up North to work with us in this. Probably we never woulda been out there tryin' to integrate if they hadn't come here. They just brought us a sight on different laws and things that we didn't know.

Will you tell us about some of the things that took place when you integrated the ice cream parlor?

VW: All I can remember now was when we got up there to buy at the bar where they didn't want us to be, the lady behind the counter just said she wadn't gonna sell us any cream. You hadda go to the side, on the outside. We wanted one take-out window, not one on the side for colored and another for whites to buy the cream. One time the night man come with his dog they was gonna put on us, tryin' to make us go 'way. But we didn't go. Wadn't too long after that, she served us finally at the front window.

They never tried to arrest y'all when you went to the ice cream parlor?

VW: No, they didn't. Just wouldn't serve us. A lot of peoples got arrested over in Lexington—our chairman, Mr. Walter Bruce, and Mrs. Bee Jenkins, and I don't know who all.

We also integrated the railroad station up here. The goal was just to integrate: We wanted to integrate everything. They had white and colored;

everything was separate at that time. They didn't allow colored folks with them in anything. But we wanted to get us together, working together, sitting together in everything.

When we first started integrating, it was just me and Arie Johnson went. We went over there an' talked to the man at the window about we wanted to integrate, and they didn't agree to it. And after we got it integrated an' they did away with the colored waitin' room, the whites don't come in there. If they go on the train, they sit in their car 'til they ready to get on. You don't ever see them sitting in the station, naw.

Were you scared that first time you went over there and sat with them?

VW: No, I ain't been scared since I first started out in '64.

Even when folks were gettin' killed?

VW: They sho' was, but I still didn't get afraid. That didn't stop me. I asked the Lord to take care o' me and just went on out there. I overcome fear by keep goin'. If I hadda stopped, I probably would've got afraid. But I kept it keepin' on

Do you know anybody who stopped?

VW: Plenty o' them; I migh' near couldn't name 'em all. When we got the Head Start—that's the first job we got for the colored—lots of 'em just broke off, and they still is not with us. After they got the Head Start job, they completely stopped comin' to the meetin's. It seemed like they wadn't interested. All they wanted was a job.

Was it hard for blacks to get jobs?

VW: When the whites were gettin' plants 'round here, they begged the color' folks to sign to get the plants. After we was in this Movement, Mary Lee Hightower went and got a job there. One night they had some boys out there was gonna do something to her. She protected hersel' and went 'n' called her uncle. After they seen him coming, they shoot, they run. After that they fired her, and she put a suit in against them.

It was hard for blacks to get jobs then. That's why we went to Washington to talk about what was going on in Mississippi, the trouble at the plant. They didn't want to hire colored. After they got the factory, they said "white only."

Who specifically did y'all talk to?

VW: To the congressmen. We went in the congressmen's room, and all around that table we was sittin'. They had me, Viola Winters, for the spokesman. I told 'em all about down here and how they did about the plants and everything. And I told how Mrs. Ida Moore over the welfare was coming in black folks' rooms and looking under the beds and see if they got mens and things under there. We marched around Washington and come home.

What were their responses?

VW: They didn't know that was going on in Mississippi. They was glad to hear it. They didn't tell us what they was goin' to do. All we know, when we got back down here, they were hiring the colored folks in the plant and they fired the lady from the welfare.

From then on we marched all around Durant and had meetings. There wasn't any black folks here voting. So we went up there in Lexington to the courthouse. We had a hard time; they had a lot of questions to keep you from registerin'. Then when we started to voting, we had a hard time doing that 'cause we had to go 'round trying to beg them to come out of the house to vote. Black folks wasn't use' to anything like this.

I was sittin' where the voting was happening when we was trying to put Representative Robert Clark in what he is now in Jackson [the first black since Reconstruction to sit on the Mississippi legislature]. We sit down and take names—how many white and colored voting. I was sittin' there one voting day, and a white man come up and told me, "Get up and get outta here!" Then I saw the pistol in his pocket. He would brush by me, trying to scare me out. But, y'see, I didn't get up. Finally, I saw Mrs. Elra Johnson come in, and I told her go get somebody to identify this man; but when she come back, he was gone.

The hardest time we had was trying to get registered. They didn't want color' folks to vote. They didn't want equal rights. They had it so long to themselves, they don't want us with them. They can't help it now.

We went to integrating the schools. We integrated the white school up there. That morning all of 'em was linin' up there in the street. They had all the polices and things on the side for them to go by. Those that wasn't afraid, they just went on through.

Hooker Riley was goin' out every Wednesday night an' workin' with us, and when they integrated the schools, he opened up his store for us to come and have a meetin'. So we went to his store and sit down and waited and told 'em if anything happened, that's where they would get us. If they needed us. But they never did need us. Some of the whites was meddlin' the children after they integrated, but that still didn't stop 'em.

After they integrated, the whites went and got 'em a private school up here in West, and there's one in Lexington, too.

Why did y'all integrate Durant Hospital?

VW: Y'see, in Durant Hospital wadn't no colored in the room with the white. They just had you in separate rooms. If the whites could sleep in the nice beds on the front, we wanted the colored folks to do that, too. We got that integrated. Had us civil rights nurses here 'n' they helped us. We just kept goin' back, an' we marched around the building and kept going and talking to 'em and to the nurses. Just bein' round there when they'd be comin' in to see the sick. We'd be watchin' 'em, see how they do. At that time they wanted the senior citizens to pay fifty dollars down to enter. We got that stopped, too.

Just so much they was doing to us. We really didn't know the law at that time; they had the law in they hand. They was just running it like they wanted to run. We had a hard time tryin' to do all that. That's why I was interested in the Civil Rights Movement. I'm still interested in it, in getting justice. That was all we want—justice. We never did have it. They always had the line in they hand.

Can you see changes? How do you feel about the way things are now compared to when you were growing up?

VW: I feel so much better the way they going now, because we doing a lot we didn't do then. We didn't use to vote, didn't sit in the railroad station where they sit. And on the train, I believe, it use' to be white folks sat in the front; we was in the back. I feel much better now it's integrated. That's what God wants. He wants us together.

How did it feel to be a black lady back then? Did you feel you weren't equal to the white lady?

VW: We wadn't equal with the white people. At that time whoever we were working for, we had to go in the back door. They didn't allow you in the front 'cause we was black [laughs]. You go to those white folks' house to cook, they make you go through the back door. Now you can go in the front door.

Wasn't that degrading, making you less of a person, having you go through the back door?

VW: Uh huh. 'Course I'm not working for them now.

Were there more women than men involved in the Movement?

VW: I always think it was more women, 'cause almost in everything it's more women [laughs].

What did the women do in the Movement?

VW: They did everything the mens did, yeah 'bout. We marched, went to the meetings, went to Washington—women did. Where they was, we was there, mostly. There were lots of women leaders. Rosa Parks and the lady they beat up up there in Winona, Fannie Lou Hamer. I think

Women were as important as men in the Holmes County Movement. Attending this 1965 meeting at the Holmes County Community Center in Mileston were (from left) Alma Mitchell Carnegie, Annie B. Mitchell, C. Bell Turnbow, Caldonia Davis, Mary Turnbow (standing), Florence Blackmon, Rogers Head (standing), and Maude C. Vance.

she was grand, a wonderful woman, outstanding. She wadn't afraid. She was one believed in the civil rights, knewed it, and went on towards that. I just admired her.

Was it something new for women to be so involved in the Movement?

VW: It was new in a way because it was something we never did before. And I'm still in there. I done got to age, but I'm a still stay there 'til God call me.

Did people ever want to use violence in the Movement back then?

VW: No, not really. Y'see, I was only in this Movement in Durant, and we didn't use no violence. Only one day Hooker Riley was going out to the [Community] Center, and they was out laying in the road for him, and they had their guns at him. He did shoot back at them out of his car.

And one time we was in the Second Pilgrim Rest Church and we left out of there. And they tried to burn up the church. But we found it in time before it caught on.

It wasn't maybe a month that we was goin' out there. It got so bad that our black mens had they guns and they watch the place that night. They had to be watchmen.

Were there any threats or violence against you in the Movement?

*Fannie Lou Hamer speaks to
1969 Freedom Democratic
Party rally inside Holmes
County Courthouse.*

VW: As I told you, some man came in front of me with a gun. He didn't do nothing, but it was something unusual to me. An' then they come along and throwed eggshells and things in your yard. Just aggravate.

And one threat was this: I took in a white lady called Harriet. She was here working with us. I brought her down here to stay all night, and she had a check she wanted to cash. I told her, "Let's go up town." Wouldn't nobody cash her check. And then that evening the police come and sit on the side of the road right there by the window. We just watched him, see what he gonna do. He didn't do anything, 'less only to threat. . . . They burned crosses at folks' houses.

What was the purpose of them burning crosses?

VW: Because o' meanness. They just didn't like the way we was doin' to get this thing integrated. They were tryin' to scare us, break us up from integratin' or havin' meetings. That's all I know it could be.

Were you worried about them burning crosses?

VW: I wadn't worried about it. They never did put one here. They put one at Arie Johnson's house. It didn't stop her either. An' they put one at Mr. Blanton's house when he was in Washington with us. We called him C. H. Blanton. We thought they would never put one at his house. He was a white man.

So how did he get involved with y'all?

VW: He was the mayor at that time. He went to Washington with us. I guess he went to see how it was gonna be. While he was there, they burned a cross at his house. It was very often they had crosses at people's houses.

Was anything ever done to those folks who were burning crosses?

VW: They never did have nothing done to them.

Did anyone even investigate it? And what about the shooting at Hooker Riley's?

VW: Naw, naw. Never took it into court.

Where did all the hate come from that whites feel toward blacks?

VW: It might come from back there in slavery on up. They always've been like this. 'Cause we all know white folks never did like color' folks and didn't wanna be around them. If you don't be around a person, there's nothing you can do. They never did treat us like we were human.

Does it sometimes upset you that blacks do not vote today, after all you went through in the Movement to get blacks able to vote?

VW: It kinda worry me, but I realize that black folks ain't never had nothing. Seem like some don't even want nothing. They still out there with the white man. A lot of 'em right now will carry messages back to him.

What else do you think needs to be done? Or is the Movement finished?

VW: I don't think it will ever be finished. It's a whole lot—I just can't name all that need to be done. I think if we could just come together, it would be much better; we could get a lot done. We is not together like we should because a whole lot of 'em [who] started with us is not with us now. They are gone home and sat down. They don't come to the meetings like they use' to. Until we as a black race do something about it, nothing gonna get better.

MR. ROBERT COOPER HOWARD

"They Wanted Me Bad"

JEFFREY BLACKMON & FELISHA DIXON

It was a hot July day when we drove to Goodman to interview Mr. Cooper Howard. Our teacher dropped us off at a white frame house. Mr. Howard already had chairs arranged outside in the shade. His wife, Mrs. Lillie Mae Howard, sat with us during the interview, and his son Jerry joined us now and again.

Before we began the interview, Mr. Howard probably thought that we were just kids who didn't know what we were doing. You see, he had been interviewed in years past by other kids as part of ROCC's annual essay contest on the history of Holmes County from a black perspective. We wanted our interview to be different, so we worked extra hard by doing research. We read up on previous interviews with Mr. Howard and looked up newspaper articles that featured his name. And, sure enough, after we asked the first question, a spark seemed to grow in Mr. Howard's eyes. He knew we were not just wasting his time but had done our homework.

As we interviewed Mr. Howard we discovered that he had marched and had sent his children to the white school in Goodman. Night-riders shot into his house because of his strong stance. His wife was shot in the leg, and other bullets narrowly missed the eleven children in the room. But do you think that stopped them from participating in the Movement? No! It made them work even harder. Mr. Howard believes that every person is equal. He had fought for his country in the army, and he wanted some respect.

Well, he has our respect for the way he fought for our rights. Mrs. Howard was mostly quiet during the interview, but we could tell she is a strong woman herself. There are many more things we could tell you now, but we'll let you read the interview instead. We bet you'll enjoy it as much as we did.

[In the following interview, the speakers are Mr. Cooper Howard (**CH**), Mrs. Lillie Mae Howard (**MH**), and Mr. Jerry Howard (**JH**).]

❧

Mr. Cooper Howard, could you tell me what it was like having children integrate the schools?

CH: It was kind of rough, it was kinda dang'ous, but after I made up my mind, I just went 'head on and did it. I had a hard shell. I was harassed; some of everythan' happened. They burned crosses; they put out leaflets tellin' me what I bet' do, not do; my house was shot into; my wife was shot in the right leg.

They did everythan' for me to take those children out of school, but I did not. After they went that year, all the whites left, left only eighteen li'l blacks up there. And they stayed there the whole year.

You say someone burned a cross in front of your house?

CH: Yeah, they had cross burns right in front of my house. If they hadda put that cross on this side of the road, it was gonna be a lot of trouble. I was looking at them when they was nailing it down an' everythang and saw them when they throw the match to it. I didn't say nothin' to 'em. They burned one here at the church and one in the fork where y'all turn off up here. I call the sheriff about nine o'clock and you know what time he came to see about me? Three o'clock the next evening. He said, "Cooper, what happened?"

I said, "Sheriff, look like to me you don't care what happened. I called you last night at nine o'clock, an' you just now gettin' here. It would've did you good to come here an' look down on me burned up!" I said, "The very next one come up and do something in front of my house, I will be calling the undertaker!"

When they fired into my house, I just happen to be out here, and I fired right back on 'em. That's the way I caught 'em, 'cause I had got the word they was coming by that night to get me. That was Halloween night in 1965. I was waitin' on 'em, and they came by. They throwed two cherry bombs, a smoke bomb, stink bomb or something. But I had my automatic shotgun settin' right at the front door, and I fired up through that oak tree there to let 'em know I was at home.

'Bout an hour after that, they eased by, went back up there, turned around and came back. I had gone out, got myself stationary. They went up, made three trips. That third trip's when they fired into the house. Shot in. You can see the holes in the window and in the siding of the house there. I got a bed in there where the bullets went all in that bed. My wife was shot in the knee; the bullet's still in there now. All my children was back in that room. I had eleven children in that same room that my wife was shot in.

Then they came right on by me, and just as they got to me, I started to firin' on 'em. Some of them shots hit 'em. One boy, I know, got a load in the arm. There were several more in the car.

They carried my wife on to the hospital. They didn't put me in jail at the time. They set me out in front of the courthouse. It was about eleven or twelve o'clock that night, and I set right there in front of the jailhouse in the sheriff car till six o'clock that mornin' before they carried me down to jail. Say, "You done shot them fellows, and we gonna put you in jail."

I say, "Yeah, but I was at home tending to my business when they come shootin' into my house. I wadn't out there meddlin'; they come there meddlin' me. I think I had a right to shoot back at them done shot int' my house." So finally they up and let me out.

That next mornin' the sheriff sent his deputies here and take all the guns we had. I told 'em we was tryin' to protect ourselves, just as everybody else protect theirs. They take my gun. I told 'em I was gonna buy me some more guns. "You can take ever' one I buy, but I gonna protect my family. I live here, I'm paying taxes here, I'm not botherin' nobody." Simply 'cause those two little boys was going to the white school over there.

Martin Luther King talked about nonviolence, but you shot back. How did other civil rights workers react to that?

CH: They was behind my back all the way, but I don't figure that I was violent. All I was doin' was protectin' myself. You see, if you gonna fight me, why 'ontcha come face to face? Why slip around at night sneakin' around and do it? See, the onliest way to break the sneakin' around at night is you gonna have to get ready for it. They would sneak around and then laugh about it.

But it happen they got caught that time, and that absolutely stopped it. Haven't been any more nightriders and bombin' peoples at night, goin' down their houses, burnin' crosses, doin' things. That broke all that up. I figure like this: Somewhere down the line somebody had to do somethin' to stop it. If they hadn'a did it, they would've been doin' it yet.

I didn't bother nobody, pick at nobody—only thang I was wantin' was *equal justice*, just like everybody else. An' why is it that I go to the army, served in Uncle Sam's army three years and four months, then come back and be treated as if I hadn't went? And I figure that if I can go int' Uncle Sam's army to try an' fight for America, I can come back and be counted as an American. Not as somebody that's throwed aside.

I felt that you're in your house, ain't botherin' nobody, the only thang you hunting is equal justice. An' they gonna sneak by at night, burn your house, or shoot in there. And you gonna sit there and take all of it? You got to be a very li'l man with no guts at all. I would get threatened, telephone calls. All kind of threats. The sheriff told me I should get my people together and carry 'em back to Africa where they come from. I told him I'll make a deal: "If you get your people and carry 'em back and give the Indian back the land you taken, I might." I say, "I'm a American-born black man. I have no other place to go but here. Ain't but one more place and that's at Hillcrest Cemetery."

So did that make you mad, or what?

CH: Oh yeah, it made me pretty warm. I got pretty mad.

Did it ever make you want to go shoot up folks?

CH: I just didn't want to go out and shoot 'em up, but I figure like this: If they try to attack me, then I was goin' to protect myself. And that's in me today. I'm not gon' meddle, but I want you to treat me like you want to be treated. I'm human like you; the only thang we just got a different color, but I'm a man just like you. I'm entitle' to what God put here on earth just like you is entitle' to it.

Do you think if your children hadn't gone to the school that you wouldn't have been messed with?

CH: Oh yeah, they were gon' mess with me. They wanted me bad. I was on the wanted list. *I was wanted.* They wanted to destroy me because I was standin' up for what was right for black people. I was participating with the Civil Rights Movement, tryin' to get people to move forward, because they had freedom like anybody else. It was time for 'em. Now was the time to walk on out, to show theirselves as men and women and be as citizens of Holmes County.

Did you take your children out of school?

CH: No! No! No! There was about one hundred and twenty-six children that had signed up to go to school over there. When it come down to the children comin' up there, only eighteen li'l children went up there. But if the rest of 'em hadda went. . . .

Did your children ever just not want to go?

CH: Nah, those boys wanted to go. They never was afraid; none of my children never was afraid. I had one kind of afraid; but the rest of 'em, ever' move I would make, they was right there with me.

Edna, she was one of the fighters back in the '60s. She got locked up down there in Jackson. They had them down there at the state fairground, fenced in like pennin' cows. Edna told them, "Why are you putting us in a pen like you put hogs and cows?" They had that thing fenced all round.

Two hundred Holmes Countians marched in Jackson in June 1965, and over one hundred were jailed at the state fairgrounds. Pictured here are teenagers Sandra Hayes, Vernice Clark, and Sonja Fort with outside volunteer Sue Lorenzi as they march in front of the Old Capitol Building just before being arrested.

The judge told them when I went to pick up my daughter and Mrs. Hattie Boyd's daughter, "If I don't catch 'em back down here, this is their freedom." I told him, "If they want to be locked up down here, then that is their freedom!" Edna say she really enjoyed it. The police was trying to shut them up. They was just sanging, having a good time when I got down there.

Were your parents involved in the Movement?

CH: My daddy was deeply involved. And he lived to get just two months offa being ninety-nine years old. He would go to just about every meetin' I would go to. He was right there. And you see that boy right there [nods at his son Jerry]? He marched. Happened in Grenada, was it?

JH: That was the big march Martin Luther King had. I marched from Sardis Dam all the way to Jackson. When they got into Canton and put us up that night, they sprayed us with that tear gas.

CH: We marched right into Tougaloo College. We marched look like twenty miles around Jackson. But when we got to the State Capitol building, there was men with shotguns all the way around. They wouldn't let us in there. They had us surrounded with guns to keep us away from there. But Dr. King made his speech out there. There were white people right out of Goodman standin' aside, watchin' who was from Goodman in that march.

That was the march with James Meredith? So they came right down Highway 51?

CH: Right!

Do you remember Stokely Carmichael from SNCC on that march?

CH: Stokely Carmichael, right. He was the one would pull down the Rebel flag. Every time he just take a little boy and put him up there and have him get that flag down and stick an American flag up there.

Were his speeches different from Dr. King's?

CH: Much different. It were just a good speech. In other words, Dr. King brought it about in a religious way. An' Stokely Carmichael brought it out like it should be. He brought the whole works out—what were different between the white and black. Then he talked about the governor, saying, "The governor oughtta be here." He could talk, too. And James Meredith made a good speech about the schools.

And I was in the first march that they performed here in Holmes County to get people registered. We had about two hundred people 'cause the rest of the people was just afraid. They was sayin' what was goin' to happen was that we goin' to get killed. The white people goin' to kill us.

Well, I figure like this: I went to taking my basic training in Aberdeen, and I marched on that soil. Then I marched down there to Flora, Mississippi. I was up to Savannah, Illinois; I marched there. Then I was shipped to California; I marched there. Then went over to Hawaii, and I marched there.

So if I can march in the army where they fightin' at, surely if this is a free country, I can march here. If you can march in those places, why not come home and march some? And so that's the way I felt about it. When they say, "March," I was right there. I just loved to march because I marched in the army.

But that's when they had the old dogs. That German Shepherd dog, he was at the door, and he would bite. And see, then people wouldn't go in there because they knew the dog would bite.

Mr. Henry McClellan know 'bout that. He was the circuit clerk, but he would not help you or didn't want you to come in there to get registered.

And most of our professional people was scared to go in that office. They went down to the post office under federal registrars. The grassroot people went up there while it was tough, amongst the dogs and the bad sheriff and those bad people. We went up there and got registered.

You say the circuit clerk didn't want anybody to register. How did y'all manage to do it?

CH: It was by havin' the Justice Department come in and told 'em that these people had to register. Then they moved the dog back. But long as you was in there, they talked to you so bad. Talkin' to old people, tellin' 'em, "I ain't gon' help you. You can stay there and look like a coon, old possum!" He told my daddy that. My daddy were eighty year old.

So what did you do?

CH: I say not one thang 'cause if I hadda open my mouth, he woulda said something to me. Then I would've put him across the counter.

What about the FDP at that time?

CH: The FDP was very strong at that time all over the county. Community people was organized. I was the chairman of this community. I worked hard to keep people together, and when it was time to march, I would have people to go marchin'. I just go and talk to 'em. I never quit goin'.

People use' to tell me, "Stay home, it's dangerous to be out." But I figured this: My business had to be seed after. If I get killed, I just done get killed. I'm gonna get killed for what's right. But we had no building to meet in. We'd meet up at my daddy's and mother's. And people from all over the county would come to the meetings. Now, y'all may think it's a joke, but when people would walk at night, they'd have pen knives, axes, long knives, and everything to protect them. They was scared somebody was gonna attack them.

Now, when I leave to go to a meetin', my oldest boy would sit right here with an automatic shotgun across his lap. He would guard 'til I got back. I would take half of the night, and he would take the other half. My daddy-in-law was here, all my people live here, and they ain't gonna take no foolishness. I had a brother, Dilly. He was dangerous. He was really tough. I had to talk to him. Ain't no joke—he was ready.

Mr. Howard Taft Bailey, Reverend Barnett, an' a guy by the name of Emmett White stayed here a whole week with me. We sat on the hill, back to back, waiting all night long.

How did you overcome your fears?

CH: My fear just finally grew out of me. I had made up my mind: I would die and go to hell before being treated like a dog. I had faith the Almighty would protect me. Right gonna win. But I believe in fighting now; I'll fight in a minute, because you young people haven't saw what I saw in my time. There was a man down here they put in jail, and the Ku Klux went down an' shot that man to pieces. I have saw men hung behind cars and drug. I've saw people walk down the

Goodman Street an' get push' off and beat to death by white people. And black people stand there lookin' at 'em.

Mrs. Howard, were you ever scared?

MH: Me and Jerry never was scared.

Were you gonna shoot back?

MH: Yeah!

Can you shoot a gun?

MH: Yeah!

During Freedom Summer, did any freedom riders stay with you?

CH: I had freedom riders to stay here. Male and female.

Where did they sleep?

CH: Some in the beds, on the floor, anywhere they felt like it. They had a sleeping bag; just spread something on the floor an' lay on it.

How long did they stay with you?

CH: 'Bout a month or two.

Did the freedom riders help around the house?

CH: Yeah, they was very smart. They would help an' come out in the yard with the children, playing with the little ones.

How did local whites react to that?

CH: They didn't like it. They would ride by here looking, and say, "Them long-hair folks staying at Cooper Howard's!" Some stayed with my sister. I wasn't afraid to let them stay here. They human!

Did they give you any money to help buy food and stuff?

CH: They would buy their own food. Most time we would give 'em breakfast, and rest of the time they have their own. I was glad for them to be in here 'cause they was opening people's eyes to what you was entitled to.

How did the freedom riders really change things, if you were already doing it? If they never had come in, would you have tried to vote?

CH: Oh yeah, we had decided we was gonna do it. But we would have went up and got turn away. Never would have got redished [registered]. We would have been in the same fix, like back in slavery. But those people had the backin' of the NAACP, SNCC, COFO. They had a lawyer from the president's office.

By having your own three acres of land, was that a big help back then?

CH: Yeah, I never did suffer. A lot of people were put out of where they were working. Take the schoolteacher who could not participate in

SNCC or anything concerning civil rights. Bernice Montgomery was the only teacher that stood up. When we got the school integrated, the schoolteachers begun to come out, but they still don't come out like they should.

I think the teachers should be some of the leading people out there. They supposed to be out there looking for you, opening your eyes to what's happening. And you don't have a preacher hollerin' in any pulpit but mine.

What about in the Movement?

CH: No Lord, you couldn't hardly get a preacher. Very few would come out. You would see no preacher an' schoolteacher. They wouldn't let you have a meeting in their church. Your grassroot people are the ones that opened this thing up and got it going—people who wadn't scared. They just opened the doors for people to walk in.

But the white folks are working the trick all the time to get you back from where I just came from, in slavery. If a lot of people don't wake up, they gonna be right back down.

So you know something to do to defend ourselves from going back?

CH: Yeah, by working together, talking to your leaders—your preacher, your schoolteacher. Those are the people depending on you for a living. If you didn't go to school, the teacher wouldn't get paid. If you didn't go to church, the preacher wouldn't get paid. They got to move out in front, teach this thang to you.

Putting your dollar together. If you got to buy from that man out there, then you are going back down. Take me, I got my own cows. I can make it on my own, if it ain't nothin' but cows. We can buy some land, raise hogs, pea patch, all that kind of stuff. Then you don't have to depend on somebody else.

By telling young people to get involved 'cause all the old fighters is dying. Now where that gonna leave y'all? The young people should have a voice like the old people. Let them speak their opinion. If they speaking wrong, chastise 'em and tell them what's right.

MRS. ANNIE WASHINGTON

*School Integration
Through the Eyes of a Child*

WILLA WILLIAMS & RODERICK WRIGHT

M rs. Annie Washington resides in Pickens, Mississippi. We thought she was a good person to interview because she was a young black child who tried to integrate a white school in the 60's in Goodman, a neighboring town of Pickens; we felt we needed someone with this perspective to complete our book. Mrs. Washington was very cooperative when we called and asked to interview her.

Mrs. Washington (formerly Annie Williams) is in her early thirties. She is about five feet four inches tall. Her facial features include brown eyes with a sort of twinkle about them. She has a very sure look. You can see that she is proud of how she integrated the school as a child. Before she talks, she takes a pause to consider her words. She is intelligent and confident of herself and her capabilities.

Mrs. Washington is a mother of three: an eighth grader and twins that are in first grade. She smiles a lot, but she is a serious person when it comes down to her children; she seems very concerned about their future. Her current occupation is as elementary school librarian at Goodman-Pickens Elementary School.

Mrs. Washington was kind of nervous when we and the CBS camera crew showed up. Roderick and I were also nervous. But Mrs. Washington just welcomed us, and at that moment we began to feel comfortable. She is someone who we think really stands out among people because of her courage and determination.

[In the following interview, **AW** is Mrs. Annie Washington.]

To start off, I would like to ask you what year did school integration begin?

AW: [The year was] 1965, if I'm not mistaken. They desegregated first through fourth grades, and there was one black child in kindergarten, but he wasn't really being taught.

What was the name of the school?

AW: The only thing we ever knew it as was Goodman School. As a part of Holmes Junior College.

The building that you actually went to school in, is it still standing?

AW: Yes, they're using it for the boys' dorm. It's across Highway 14, the big brick building.

Did you go back the second year?

AW: No, I didn't. The Goodman-Pickens Elementary School opened that next fall, and that's where everybody went after the first year at the white school.

Where did the older white children go?

AW: The older white children, I think they left and went to a private school; they didn't stay with us.

Did you hear your mother and father talking about you going to the school, or did you want to go?

AW: I never heard them say anything, but I didn't want to go because I was leaving my friends. I didn't know if white people were gonna be there and how it was gonna be. I really didn't have a choice in the matter, either way it went. A lot of black children were supposed to go; but I guess when school started, they just backed out. They were afraid of what would have happened because, at that time, there were a lot of threats to the black parents, if they would send their children there. I guess the ones that sent theirs just didn't care about threats. And we were threatened after we got there. There were eighteen of us—three from where I lived on Howard's Hill and the rest of them came from across town; that's in Goodman.

Were Aaron Malone's children going?

AW: Yes, three of them, if I'm not mistaken. I remember Marie, Aaron, and William. There were two different classes in the school—one for grades one through two, and one for three through four. And grades one through two were taught by a Mrs. Jones, and the class for three through four was taught by Mrs. Kilebrew. They were both white.

How did the other students feel about you coming into the school?

There wasn't anybody [whites] there. We were the only ones. But evidently they didn't like it because they moved out. They went to a private school.

How did you feel when you first went to this school?

AW: I talked to my mama earlier this morning, and I told her I couldn't remember anything about the first day there. And she told me they carried us up there, and all eighteen of us children seemed to have been very afraid. She even mentioned that, for that one day, there were a few white children there. But I guess after they saw that we were gonna stay, they moved out.

Every day at school it was nice, peaceful. Everything was fine. I felt good, until them college students would come over. On several occasions the teachers would leave during our lunch time, and the white college students would come, and they would get big iron baseball bats and baseball sticks. And because we were so small, we had no protection. So we would run into the woods to try to get away from them. Also, they would come during our recess time. The teachers would be there, but they wouldn't say anything. They would just let them run us and do whatever they wanted. And that makes you not wanna go to school because you felt the same thing was gonna happen the next day. One girl had an incident once trying to get away from them, but she wasn't seriously hurt. Those college students had us all afraid, even the boys. But they were only small boys.

They picked on y'all because you were small or because they thought they could get away with it?

AW: During that time it could have been because of three things: [First], they could have gotten away with it. Who could have pinpointed them? We didn't know their names. We couldn't identify them. So if they had harmed us, nobody would have told anybody about it. [Second], we were small, and that was an advantage to them. And [third] we were black, and it was a problem during that time.

And sometimes after we had told the teachers and they had seen the students coming there for themselves several times, you think they would have tried to do something. But they never did. So it was like we were just there. They didn't care. Usually when I think back to when I was in school, I can remember something about being taught. The only thing I can remember there was math.

It was a touch-and-go situation. We even had the chance to leave campus, which we weren't supposed to do. Our parents didn't know about it until later in the year. But they [teachers] would leave, didn't care if we left or not, and we would always go downtown. And because we were so small, that was dangerous. It stopped when the white merchants started complaining about us being unsupervised coming in their stores. Probably because we were black; plus they knew that we were coming from the white school.

Do you think that some of the people that probably seem nice as can be now may have been the students who were after you all the time?

AW: Yeah! I got a feeling that they are still in Goodman, somewhere in that area; but I just don't know.

Do you think they have changed?

AW: No! I think it's been instilled in them from childhood up, and I don't think there's any way to get it out. Maybe there was some way when they were smaller; maybe it could have been erased.

Do you think the incidents with the college students could have been prevented if y'all were bigger?

AW: No, because it still would have been more of them than us. And that probably would have been an even bigger problem—a few of us going against the biggest of them. Then the next time they're gonna bring somebody different to fight you. We didn't have anybody to come there and do for us. Our big sisters and brothers were in the other school. And another thing: Our parents taught us against fighting. So I'm sure if the students hit us, our parents wouldn't have wanted us to hit back. Just come and report it; then they would take steps from there.

So you all were nonviolent people?

AW: Nonviolent. I believe that no one group of people were put here to rule. Nobody is more than anybody. Everybody should love one another as they love themselves. If we did that, we would be able to get along better. There wouldn't be any prejudice. There would never have been anything such as integration or segregation. I went there. I was hurt by the things the white children did. And even when I think about it today, it hurts. But I can't hold it against 'em, I can't. And I don't think there's anything I would do to try and get back at any other white for what happened to me then. If I had white children in the classroom, I would treat them as I would treat my own. Because I have three, and I would want them to get the best.

On an affidavit I read that when you and your sister got ready to ride the bus, the flag boy just passed on by you, like you weren't supposed to get on.

AW: Yes, they just went straight on past, like I wasn't there. Didn't want us to ride it, but the next day they did stop.

And with riding the bus, that was really hurting, knowing that there were only four of us blacks on that bus and the rest white. And they were much bigger—I think they were high school students. They would threaten us with what they would do to our bodies if we ever got on the bus again. And they would always make us go to the back of the bus to sit. It had gotten so bad at one point that my father had to go meet the bus driver to tell him that he wasn't gonna have that, and that if anything happened to me, he would have to take action. I remember an incident did happen with the Malone children where they gummed their hair and clothes and things. I'm not sure what their father did about it.

I lived about a mile from school, but a lot of days they [my parents] would send me to the road to catch the bus; but because I was afraid to get on, I wouldn't. I would walk down the hill and wait until the bus passed. Then I would go to my uncle's house and go with his son and nephew. We would walk to school by ourselves. And in the evening time we would walk home. A lot of times the bus would come on the edge where we were, and we would have to get off in the ditch to keep from being ran over.

When these people were picking on you on the bus, what did the bus driver do?

AW: Nothing. I felt he was a part of it. There was a young man here from New York, Bob Coleman, during that time, and my parents told him what was going on. He was one of the civil rights leaders, Movement people, that came to help us, and he carried me over to my aunty's house and put me in a room by myself with him. He put on the tape recorder and told me to tell everything I could remember about it. I was afraid to do so because he was white, and I thought he would take everything I say and give it to the white people that really wanted to hurt us. But finally, in my words as a child, I told him just what had happened on the bus with me.

A lot of times when you sit up and think about it now, do you ever feel like integrating the schools again if you have to?

AW: After I talked to Willa last Friday, that question came to mind. If my children had to be put in a predicament like that, would I do it? And it's a hard question to answer, because even today we still have them same problems. It's getting better, but under cover things are kind of the same, yes. So I would be skeptical about doing that. If they wanted to, it would be their choice. But I don't think I would. Maybe in time I would change; but right now I just don't know, because I don't want them to be put through what I went through. I was a child; I couldn't protect myself. I didn't really understand what was going on. You know, at that age you think everybody should be able to get along; but I found out differently, and even today in some places it's the same way. I believe that if I had to have stayed at that school another year, it would have been hard. I probably would have wanted to drop out in fifth grade. At one point they thought we had to go back that next year, because part of the school that we transferred to wasn't finished. The restrooms weren't completed, but they bought two outdoor units, and they let us in anyway.

I remember black kids used to always talk about us because we went to this white school; they had this thing about the Howards, and the biggest of the children that went there were related to the Howards. It was hard to get them to see that *they* had a chance to go too; but for some reason their parents rejected it and wouldn't let them go. So in a sense, we got it from both races—black and white. They didn't understand why we could go and they didn't go. But it wasn't our fault; it was their parents' fault.

Did a bus come and pick you all up at the school you transferred to?

AW: Yes, the same bus that would come by to pick up our older sisters and brothers when we were in the white school. We even tried several times to get on that bus, but he [the bus driver] wouldn't let us on because he said it was against the policy; we weren't going to that school so we couldn't ride the bus.

So your older sisters and brothers were going to a high school?

AW: Yes, because the white school stopped at fourth grade. It didn't take on anything else. You had to go to the old school—the school that is now William-Sullivan High in Durant. It used to be called the Durant Attendance Center. And the school in Goodman we used to call the Goodman Old School. That's where I went for the first three years.

Do you see any hope in the future?

AW: That's a good question. There is hope, because there are the good; and I think the good outnumber those that don't care. If you take those that are good, it will be a good future—black and white will be together. That's something I am hoping for.

Do you think one day in Holmes County whites and blacks will go to school together?

AW: I hope so. Maybe that way we can all become one—not two, just one. I think there is a chance for them to be integrated. Because of many things in the school system now. There are not many white teachers in the public schools, but they are gradually moving in. And I think that once some of them get into the system, then some of the children will come back and up to school with them.

Do you think you could have made it through at the white school if your friends were there with you to join hands and go with you?

AW: Sure, if there would have been more black children—and I believe that some of the whites would have stayed—we would have been able to make it and keep the college students from coming on campus. Parents could tell you one thing at home; but once you get to school, it's a different story. Your parents don't have to know what's going on unless you just go back and tell them. But if you know that they are prejudiced and they don't want you to fool with me, or me to fool with you, then I wouldn't go back and tell them. We could be secret friends. Then one day it's going to come out where we can be friends in the light.

MS. MURTIS POWELL

On the Front Lines of Battle

MARVIN NOEL & RODERICK WRIGHT

Murtis Powell, Marvin's grandmother, is a powerful woman in her mid-fifties. With dark skin, curly hair, small eyes, and a round face, she is strong and sturdy. She lives outside the country community of West, Mississippi, in a small house with three neat bedrooms full of double beds. From her front porch, Ms. Powell has a good view of the woods across the road. But during the Movement she lived on a white man's place. She has raised eleven kids of her own and now keeps some of her grands.

Ms. Murtis was not a big leader in the Movement, but she was on the front lines no matter how dangerous it got. She showed that action speaks louder than words. She was one of the first to send her children to integrate the white public school in Durant in the fall of 1965. Her name was on a list that was printed up and stuck on light poles all over town so whites could retaliate against those trying to integrate the public schools.

Ms. Murtis was teargassed when she marched with Dr. Martin Luther King, Jr., in the Meredith march of 1966 from Memphis to Jackson. She was also teargassed when she went to Greenville and occupied the air force base with striking sharecroppers. She isn't a big talker, but she can sure sing those freedom songs.

[In the following interview, **MP** is Ms. Murtis Powell.]

How did you first get involved in the Civil Rights Movement?

MP: By goin' to civil rights meetings, they called it FDP, the Freedom Democratic Party. We use' to meet out there at the Old Pilgrim Rest school. And we was having meetings at Durant in people's homes, talk about different things that should be done.

So what were you trying to get people to do?

MP: At that time weren't too many of 'em registered; they was tryin' to get them registered to vote.

Could you tell us about the first time you went to register to vote?

MP: Larry, a civil rights worker, took me down there. I left the freedom school and went down to tł. courthouse to register to vote. Henry McClellan didn't tell us nothing after I had finished the application. Later on he called and told Larry and 'em to tell he think I had passed the test.

Was that during Freedom Summer when all those volunteers came?

MP: It was then, yes, 'cause Larry, he took me down there. Larry was a civil rights worker what come in here and stayed with Preacher and Virgie.

Did y'all have any civil rights workers staying with you?

MP: Naw, we didn't have none staying with us during that time 'cause we wasn't on our own place then. We was living on a white man's place 'n' they didn't want 'em to come in there. But we use' to let 'em come in there and eat. They stayed around with my children, but they never did stay in the house.

It seems to me that most of the people who got involved owned their own land; but you were living on a white man's place, and he must have been able to put you off if he wanted to.

MP: Yeah! He could have put my daddy off, but my daddy just always would speak his mind. Like, they had a little summer school over there at Old Pilgrim Rest—a little freedom school. And we took our children out of the field and let 'em went to school. And my mama, she'd be scared, said the white man gonna raise the devil 'bout taking these children out of the field. My daddy always say, "These children ain't borrowed nothing from the white man; I borrowed it." And we'd send 'em to school and the white man didn't say nothing, sho' didn't. I had five and they was big enough to go to the field, but I took 'em out 'n' sent 'em to school. And Larry and Bruce use' to pick 'em up every morning and take 'em out there.

They had a freedom school here, and it was one down there by Tchula somewhere 'cause Larry and Bruce 'n' 'em use' to take my children down there. They say one night they was coming home when they had a bus full of children, and somebody got behind them down there by Tchula and followed 'em all the way home. And they had to run the bus fast and when they outrun 'em, they got up to the church over here, and say the only way they got 'way from them, they had to turn and got down in there where the cemetery's at now. And then, Bruce, he slipped out and went back down to Mattie Pearl and called Mr. Link Williams and Vanderbilt Roby 'n' them from Old Pilgrim Rest to come see about 'em. They say the car what was following them just kept on past the church.

Were all your kids scared?

MP: Yeah [chuckles], them chillun was hollerin'.

Why did you send your children to the white school?

MP: In 1965 Larry and 'em aksed me would I be willin' to let my children go into the white school. I told 'em if anybody else let theirs go, I would let mines go. Weren't too many of us let 'em went in there, nobody but Mrs. Preacher Saffold and John Allen Wright, and my sister Elouise—we was the only ones that let 'em went in the white school.

So what ya'll were doing was trying to get enough blacks together to integrate the white school? Why was it that so few of 'em were willing to do that?

MP: Didn't none of 'em want them in. There was another girl, a white civil rights worker, stayed with Preacher. She was named Donna. And me and her used to go from door to door, talk to the black people, see would they let them. All of them told us, "No, we gonna let our children stay where they s'posed to be at."

They must have been afraid of the whites?

MP: Uh huh, they was, most of them was.

How many did you send?

MP: Four, at Durant High. Mary was tenth and Bobby was ninth and Earl was third or fourth. Billy was in the fifth grade, I know.

Was it hard on them?

MP: Yeah, they say it was hard [laughs].

Did anything ever happen?

MP: Naw. I aksed them, "How was the school?" Every time they'd come back, they tell me, "It's hard, its hard. Them teachers know they's mean to us." They say they had a hard time over there in them school.

Did the other students, the white kids, meddle [with] them?

MP: Yep. They say the white kids wouldn't even 'ssociate wid them.

Did the whites stay in there, or did they leave when y'all black kids started going?

MP: Most of 'em, ya know, left and come up here to West an' put their children in this private school at West.

Did some whites stay?

MP: Yeah, some of 'em stayed, them that wasn't able to leave. It really wasn't too many there after they put those black kids in there.

THE FOLLOWING ARE NAMES OF PARENTS AND/OR GUARDIANS OF CHILDREN INTER-GRATING THE DURANT PUBLIC SCHOOL:

Barbara Carroll	Odelle Durham
Lillie Mae Cox	Eula McGee
Henry D. Hill	Albert Patterson
Amanda Ellis	Meetis Powell
Ruth Sara Hill	Mildred Coffey
Mary Louise Ellis	Ellowise Power
Laura Cox	Annie Mae Robinson
Rowertha Glover	Hattie B. Saffold
Lillie Mae Cox	Connie Bell Wright
Annie Lee Green	Jimmie Higgins
Katie Mae Griggs	Bessie Mae Huntley
Martha Hightower	Nathaniel Bailey
Annie Dora Eskridge	Elnora Lewis
Zebedee Larry	Curtis Lee Carter
Andrew Durham	Pearlie C. Carter
Sarah Artin	John Allen Wright

FIGURE 3 *Flier distributed by the KKK around Durant, September 1965. Note Ms. Murtis Powell's misspelled name.*

Did your children want to go to the school?

MP: Naw, they didn't want to go.

How did you feel about sending your kids to a white school?

MP: I felt funny in the beginning, but after mines wasn't goin' to be the onliest ones going, then I was all right about it. But my daddy never did want 'em to go there [laughs]. He'd say, "Y'all going to send them children over there to get killed. Why won't y'all go over to get killed? Don't get the children killed."

I'd say, "Daddy, ain't nothing gonna to happen to them children." Yeah, he never did want 'em to go to the white school.

Did you know anything about the lists of names of people who had sent their black kids to a white school? Shows how people were harassed. The lists were put up all over Durant so that all the white folks could see who was integrating the school so they could try and get back at them somehow. Did you see any of those lists? Your name was on it.

MP: I never did see it, but I heard them talking about it.

Did anything ever happen to you, threats or anything like that, because you had sent your kids to the white school?

MP: Yeah, only one time. We was going to a meeting over in Durant. And we all had been to the meeting and was on our way back. It was a white lawyer; I believe they call him Mel [Leventhal].

We all was coming away from the meeting, and when we got there along by Junior Food Mart there in Durant, it was a car park and Mel was in front of us. We was ridin' with a cousin, J. L. We drove up there and J. L. say, "What going on?"

I said, "I don't know." And then we seen all them white folks around Mel's car, and they had took things and knocked the lights out of his car. They had tore his car up. We was just sittin' there, and after they did that to his car, they left then. That about the only something what ever happened.

Did anyone get hurt then?

MP: Naw, didn't nobody get hurt; they didn't bother him. They just tore his car up.

So he just drove it on home with no lights? Y'all must have been scared?

MP: Yeah, I sho' was scared. I think we all was, sho' was. I remember one night we had done been to a FDP meeting. And when we come back, walking back—we didn't have no cars and thangs like they got now. When we coming back, we saw a cross there at Link Williams's fork. They had been burning a cross there when we came from FDP that night—ret in front of his house.

Did you ever have any second thoughts when something like that happened? Did you ever wonder, "Why did I ever get involved in this? Why have I put myself and my children at risk?"

MP: Yeah, I thought about it, sho' did.

But you held strong. . . .

MP: Yeah, I hold on, I didn't never give up, 'cause after that me 'n' my sister, we went to Greenville. They just brought the bus around, and every time they come around, we followed 'em 'cause we use' to follow the FDP. They was aksing people to volunteer and go down there with 'em to protest.

And we stayed over there two weeks down there protesting. We didn't really have nowhere to sleep. We was in a old, one-room house; weren't nothing in it but some old clothing like they give away. And at night if us lay down, we would have to lay on those clothes.

And one night we went in there to lay down. The ladies just had gone to sleep; the men was on the outside. They had something like tents what they stayed under. It happened one night, when we all laid down, about twelve or one o'clock, somebody had come to the window and sprayed tear gas in there on us. That just woke everybody up in there then. Everybody woke up strangled. But we stayed on there, we stayed there and we had a hard time staying there, but we stayed there them two weeks—all but my sister, Marie; she left and come back home 'cause she got scared.

Y'all know how it feels to get tear gas put on you?

MP: Yes indeed, we got tear gas in there. They was telling us, "Get your hankies and put 'em over your nose," but everybody in there was strangled.

And we got tear gas not only that one time; we got tear gas at Canton when we was marching with Martin Luther King. We walked from Canton to Tougaloo, from Tougaloo to the Capitol in Jackson. The highway patrolmen sprayed tear gas on us in Canton and beat a load of people, too.

Was that the Meredith march in 1966? Could you tell us what that was like?

MP: [Laughs] That was hard, it sho' was. It was hot and we marched. They was singin' songs, an' some old ladies would come offa their porch and join in and help us sing and walk a little piece—little ole ladies. And then they'd turn around and go back to their house.

Were there any women in the Movement with you?

MP: Yeah, it was a lot of 'em.

The men wouldn't try to talk you out of marching because you were a woman: "You better not do that . . ."?

MP: Oh, yeah, a lot of 'em would say, "Y'all gonna get out there and get killed, and have all these children on your mama." But we never did stop going.

While you were out protesting and marching, who was at home with your younger kids?

MP: My mama and daddy.

And they was steady tryin' to talk you out of doing stuff, too? Or did they support you?

MP: My daddy, he'd support us, but my mama, she didn't much want us to do it. But my daddy, he didn't work in the Movement, but he didn't never fight against the Movement. He was kinda old, but he would keep the children. He would never tell us not to go; he'd always tell us, "Y'all go on, 'cause it'll make it better for your children."

What about your children, the ones who were old enough to understand; would they ever go on marches with you?

MP: I used to take my oldest two, Mary and Bobby, they were 'bout the biggest ones. I used to take 'em; I'd let 'em march [laughs].

What about the singing? I know you got a group and you a real good singer. Did you help lead those freedom songs?

MP: Yeah, I mostly led all the songs, and they'd join in and help, sho' did. I use' to sing, "Ain't gonna let nobody turn me around, keep on walking, keep on talking, marching up the freedom line." We use' to sing "We Shall Overcome," just a lotta songs we use' to sing in the Movement.

Was there one that had "eyes on the prize" in it?

MP: Let's see, that went, "Hold on, hold on. Keep your eyes on the prize, hold on. Paul and Silas was born in jail, had no money for to go the bail. Paul and Silas begin to shout when the jail door open and they walked out. Keep your eyes on the prize, hold on." We would just make it up and sing 'em over and over again.

Of all the people, how many really got involved in the Movement? Did most of them sit on the sidelines, or were most of them really involved?

MP: No, no. Most of them was sittin' on the sidelines.

Did that ever make you mad, ya know, because you were out there trying to change all these things?

MP: Yes indeed, sho' did, just like once we was protesting in Lexington, we was on this side protesting against the white man, and some Uncle Tom blacks had them a line on the other side protesting for the white peoples. They sho' did.

Were there many preachers who got involved in the Movement?

MP: No! Wasn't many preachers, not back in that time.

Seem like they should have been reading the Gospel; they should have been helping you.

MP: I know that's the truth, but they stayed on the outside, weren't no preachers in it—not at that time, back in them times. And a mighty few blacks. And after it had been goin' on they found out, I guess, nobody else wasn't gon' get killed, then a few of them started coming in then, after I reckon they thought all the badness was over.

Did y'all accomplish everything y'all was marching for?

MP: No, we didn't. I think it's still more to do now. It mostly look like everybody done forgot. But it's still more.

MR. SHADRACH DAVIS

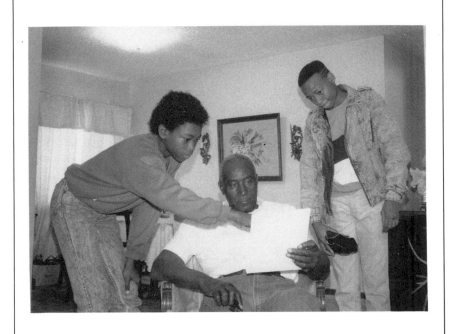

"It Don't Pay to Be Too Afraid"

THOMAS FRAZIER & NATHANIEL SPURLOCK

M̲r. Shadrach Davis lives on a dirt road in the black farming community of Mileston. He is a farmer who owns ninety-seven acres of land. He also owns an oil well that sits at the edge of his fields. He is big, healthy, and strong from working in the field almost all his life. His hands are huge. Mr. Shadrach has dark skin and talks in a rough voice. He grew up in a family of five boys and one girl. His attitude is serious; he didn't crack any jokes during the interview. He was twenty-four years old when the Civil Rights Movement started in Holmes County. Along with his neighbor, Ralthus Hayes, Mr. Shadrach gave his all to make sure that blacks gained their equal rights.

[In the following interview, **SD** is Mr. Shadrach Davis.]

How was it when you first tried to register to vote?

SD: When I first tried to go to the courthouse and register to vote, they had a man to register named Mr. McClellan, and he was very cruel. The first time I went there, I told him that I wanted to fill out an application to be a registered voter. He said, "What kinda application you want? You wanna get on the welfare?"

I said, "No, I don't. Do I look like I need welfare, huh?"

He said, "Well, you want a married license?"

I told him no, I was already married. And he stood up there for about ten minutes. He had three other white mens in the office there with him. Then he give me the application, tol' me to come on and go back round there and fill it out. And I went on round and filled it out. Then he gave me another thang to fill out which was about the constitution of the United States. And that thang was long. An' I got it and tried to fill it out to the best I could. He tol' me in fifty days I would hear from him whether I had passed or not, but I never did hear from him. I went back and filled out another one.

My mother was with me; she filled out one that same day, the first time that I went. And she passed, but he never did notify her to let her know that she'd passed. Thirteen months later, two lawyers from the Justice Department out of Washington came to our house about one o'clock one night 'n' woke her up and tol' her that they had been over there goin' over the records, and they found out that she had registered and passed fourteen months ago. And they said, "Has he notified you?"

She said, "No, he didn't. An' I went back again."

And they said, "Had you passed it then?" She said no, he didn't never inform her. Her address was on there; they wanted to know was that the address she gives.

"That sure is." How long had she been at that address?

She said, "Twenty-something odd years."

And they said, "Okay, we gon' carry them to federal court, and we're also gon' subpoena you to come to federal court down in Jackson. We want you to testify down there in federal court."

So she said, if I brought her and she were healthy, all right, she'd be glad to go. I did take her down there. And what they did when they called on her, they had her read a newspaper. She read it so far and the man stopped her, the lawyer did.

And he said, "Now, y'all hear how good this lady read in here." The other lawyer aksed her one or two questions. They let her witness.

And also Mr. Marshall who was the principal of Marshall High— they had him subpoenaed. And he had registered 'n' had passed a long time ago an' hadn't never been notified. Asked him questions, what did he do, and what was said to him 'n' all.

An' then they got McClellan in the seat and aksed him why didn't he. . . .

He said he sent that thang out, but he sent it to Carollton Young, Route 3, Lexington.

And the man said, "This paper got Route 1, Tchula. How could you . . . ?"

"I just musta made a mistake." That's what he said.

What type of questions was on the literacy test?

SD: *Took a lawyer to fill that thang out.* But those Justice Department lawyers found ninety-five whites in Holmes County that could not read and write at all and was registered. They were already registered. And the men from Washington went to visit them. They say they questioned some of 'em how did they come to be a registered voter. Said Mr. McClellan just called 'em off the streets and tol' them to come on 'n' register, and they just went on in there and he aksed 'em questions and put 'em on the book, give 'em a card that they had passed. And some—

their wives registered 'em and they didn't know nothing about it. That was the difference that they made between the races of peoples.

How many times did you try to register to vote?

SD: I tried three times. But I've known peoples that went on and tried as high as half a dozen or more times that was turned down. I think he just got tired of me comin'. You couldn't go back within thirty days, hadda give him thirty days. Quick as that thirty days up, I went right back. What they would try to do is make you get disgusted, and you just don't go back.

Then later on, they just passed a law that you go out there, and if you could read or you couldn't read, they were suppose' to help you. And folks just went to turnin' out, to goin' every day. An' that man just had to hire him a man to help all day long 'til they got the biggest portion of the people that wadn't afraid. Some people was afraid to register 'cause they was workin' for white peoples.

Plantations had quite a bit of labor livin' on 'em then; the bossman kept them afraid to go to any of our meetin's for a good while, or to go to the courthouse. And we finally had some that would get out and go to them folks' houses at night an' tell them, and finally they went to coming to the meetin's. If you's staying on one and you went to the meetin's, when the man heard about it, he tell you and your family to move immediately. He didn't want nobody on his place that registered where he could vote; he didn't need nobody that intelligent—that what he'd tell 'em.

An' I personally did everythang, talking to peoples that didn't know exactly what to do as far as registerin'. Some were hollerin', "Will I lose my job if I do this?"

"No, you ain't gon' lose your job. If enough of you go, you ain't gon' lose it. Don't but a few go, yeah. . . ." And there would be a few peoples that would go to different citizen meetin's. They lived on a plantation, or their mother was cookin' and washin'—what they call a houselady for the white person. And they find out, they fire 'em. An' the only way they could find it out was one of them Uncle Tom blacks that went to the meeting and tol' 'em that. The whites had them there to see and tell 'em to take names of everybody and what was important said at that meeting.

Did y'all do anything about the snitches?

SD: We knew some of 'em we could put our hand on, but some we didn't have enough evidence. For some we did have 'nough evidence to know who they was and let 'em know we knowed what they was doin'. That stopped 'em dere, when you let them knowed. We run one down one night an' just tol' him things he was doin' 'til he bust out an' went to cryin' an' admitted it.

Can you remember the first fourteen that registered, and share with us something about them?

SD: I can remember the very first person who held a meeting in Holmes County. They was meetin' in Greenwood, Leflore County. An' some people went from this county up there and invited them, and they would come. One of them was named Bob Moses from New York, and they had a worker named John Ball from Greenwood. We had meetin's every Wednesday night at Mileston with John Ball. When this got ready, Bob Moses came down.

Most of 'em wives went wit' 'em to the courthouse to see if they could git registered. The she'ff had 'em stand out under a tree in the yard there at the courthouse for a long time. It was late that first evenin', the first day 'fore anyone even went in, and the she'ff steady leadin' a big old collared police dog—'bout that tall [indicates three feet]. They wouldn't leave, and they let two go in to register.

They were there that whole week, from Monday through Friday, 'fore the biggest of 'em went in the courthouse. Two tried to fill out the form; I don't thank none of 'em passed it at that time. That was the first 'tempt. And the bad part 'bout it, you had a whole lotta black folk was lookin' at them folks just like they had really done a crime.

Turnbow had went to a meeting, and he went back home with his wife and daughter. After they went home and went to bed, white people came and shot in his house. They shot a firebomb in through the window; broke the window out and threw it in there. It was a ball of some kind of cloth tied really tight, soaked with coal oil.

His daughter and wife, they ran out of the house to get some water from the pump to put it out. An old man was standing out there in the yard shootin'. Turnbow was yet in the house gettin' his .22 rifle. An' when he did come out, he come out shootin'. The others shot 'cause they dug bullets outta the walls o' the house. At any rate, there was a shootout, and they say Turnbow shot one of 'em. But I know one thang: They went away from there.

And that next day he called the sheriff down there. They arrested Turnbow; said he set his own house on fire and shot in there. But they bonded Turnbow out in a couple of days.

And they also locked Bob Moses up along with Hollis Watkins and some other SNCC workers. Andrew Smith was the sheriff then. Bob Moses was down there at Turnbow's house the next day, taking pictures of what happened, and I think Andrew Smith had told him to stop; but he just kept on. Bob Moses had that camera takin' pictures, and he wadn't even payin' the sheriff a bit of attention. The sheriff twisted the camera out of his hand and taken it and then carried him on to jail.

After that, every day we would try to have some goin' from some parts of the county. And that just the way we got that thang broken down, by continually takin' peoples up there. We would have black and white law students would go up there with ya, see what happen and go in there and talk with him. Oooohh, that man would git so mad, he wouldn't know what to do.

Now, reason I didn't go [with the first fourteen], me and Ralthus Hayes kinda broke up land and planted our crops together, and he told me, "Don't you go. We don't know what's gonna happen when we go up there tomorrow; we could get hurt, some of us git killed or put in jail. But we need somebody out like you to carry on our work and to bond us out if it's necessary."

I did bond out some when they went marchin' down at Jackson [in the summer of 1965], an' they locked up all these folks from Mississippi. All those children didn't have to pay 'cause they was under-age. But Ralthus Hayes and all those was over eighteen had to pay a hundred dollars cash bond—couldn't be just a check, had to be a hundred dollars cash money. That was a whole lot of money; lot of peoples didn't have it. Those civil rights workers would call their parents and people who they knowed; some of 'em parents sent a thousand dollars for them to help bond out. They had about five busloads of 'em locked up out there where the fairground at.

It's a whole lotta people who sacrificed a lot. Back in the '50s, before the Movement, Reverend George Lee outta Belzoni was organizin' the farmers in Humphreys County [gestures to the west where the county line is, only a mile or so away]. Back then there was a whole lotta black farmers in Humphreys County. He got 'em organized. Had 'em registerin' to vote. But just like we had, they had folk goin' back and tellin' the sheriff and them what was happenin', what was bein' planned. They went to Reverend Lee and tol' him to take his name offa the voting list, but he wouldn't do it. So one evening Reverend Lee was driving home, and they shot him. His car ran into a house, and he died. That was just to scare black people from organizin'; but came a time when we was gon' be first-class citizens no matter what they done to scare us.

Yup, plenty sacrificed. When James Meredith had his march, he was shot at the beginning, and other people—hundreds of 'em—took up the march. My brother was up in Flint, Michigan. He saw all the marchin' on the television, and he couldn't stand it no more, just lookin' at what was goin' on. He had to come down. He was workin' for General Motors but came down here. Tol' me, "I want you to carry me to the march 'fore you go to the field tomorrow."

They marched right through Belzoni, had a big rally, and marched on down through Louise and the Delta and into Yazoo City and Canton. It was in Canton that they launched the tear gas on 'em. He marched all the way with 'em, all the way into Tougaloo College and Jackson. And bought foods and stuff for the children and others on the march. He couldn't bear to just see it on the television. He had to come down.

We had all kind of run-ins with the laws—laws would pick at you. And they knowed peoples like maself and a whole lot of others in the county who stayed in their own home and owned their own place. I know one night they stopped me. On Saturday nights, the civil rights workers would go over to the center, and they'd leave there and come to the store. White and black would dance together and went on. And laws—patrolmen, the sheriff, deputy, constables—would just sit there in their cars and watch. And the time you'd leave, they'd take you down the road and stop you and ask you a lotta questions.

One night I stopped in at the Mileston store a little while and got a Coca-Cola. I had already bought some bananas and some cookies— my wife was gon' make a banana pudding. I had it on the seat in the truck. He shined [his flashlight] in the truck, said, "Now what's that in the sack?"

I tol' him what it was. I knowed I wadn't speeding. He say, "Where you live?"

I say, "I live on the [Mileston] projects."

"Y'all damn project niggers think you're smart, don't you?"

I say, "Whaddya mean by smart?"

"Didn't you left away from that store while ago?"

I say, "I went out to the road, stopped, I didn't see nothing coming, I pulled out in the road. That's when you throwed that light on me and stopped me. I was driving forty miles an hour." He looked at my license and handed it back to me. It was about eleven-thirty that night out there; nobody but me and him in the road. He had two, three more in the car with him, but didn't nobody get out.

"Take your hat off and turn your light off."

I said, "What am I gon' take my . . . ?"

"Just do what I said do." I took my cap off, held it in my hand. I already gave him my license. I went on home.

That Monday I went on up there to see the mayor of Tchula. The mayor had a Western Auto store. I said, "I worked all day Saturday picking cotton with the cotton picker. I was on my way back. I stopped at Mileston store and got a Coca-Cola. When I went out to get in my truck to come on home, trouble was following me down there by that gin and stopped me and stopped another young man, too." I say, "We gonna have a big story to read about." I tol' 'em, "It be a time enough

*FDP candidate Ralthus Hayes
campaigns for county supervisor
at July 4, 1967, rally. One of
the earliest and strongest Movement leaders, Mr. Hayes died
from a stroke later that year
while on a fundraising trip to
California for the FDP.*

when it hit the paper and television. I'm just 'bout sick and tired of
'em. I don't bother nobody 'cause I work; you can't go git somethang
for yo' family an' come back home without being harassed by them."

I never did have no mo' trouble out of patrollers or the she'ff either,
but we would have to watch different ones' houses here at night. They'd
be done come burnt some crosses somewhere not too far from where
we was having a meetin', where you'd had to pass when you was leavin'.
Two or three 'f us would set in the trucks wit' guns at this driveway.
Then we'd leave an' ride over to other areas of the community—one
and two o'clock at night—'n' see how was everythang goin'.

When were you most afraid?

SD: You want to hear the truth—I never was afraid. Sho' wadn't. I
reckon that's the reason nothing didn't happen; I wadn't afraid.

It use' to be a man up the road who died, Ralthus Hayes. He was
a big civil rights man, and we use' to go from here to Holly Springs
to meetin's—that's up there not too far from Memphis. And come back
two, three in the morning. He had a truck, his daughter had a car, his
son had a car, and I had a truck and car. And we'd go in a different
one. Like tonight, if we went somewhere in this truck, tomorrow night
we'd be in a different one to try to keep them from just directing the

one what to look for, what we was ridin' in. But we never was even stopped.

Now one night Ralthus got a call from Greenwood, and it was that the white folks tried to hire his next-door neighbor to go over to Ralthus's house an' set it afire, kill him, or do something to him. He got a call from Greenwood asking him did he know this man. Ralthus say, "Yeah! He just live ret next door. His daughter and my baby girl 'long the same age; they go to school." Say, "She goes to the meetin's wit' me and my daughter."

[The Greenwood caller told Ralthus], "Well, I got a call." And this call come all the way from New York or Washington, either one. An' that evening he [the neighbor] was drivin' a tractor on up this road for a white man. We sent a man to pick him up. He'd walked from where he was workin'. We brought him on by there; we all met there on the porch of Ralthus's brother's house. We aks him had anybody tried nothing.

"Naw, ain't nobody said nothing."

"Now, you ret sho'?"

"Naw."

I say, "Well, I tell you what; we got a call today that you had been aksed. They didn't say whether you was gonna do it." Say, "But now you sayin' you ain't been out. We don't believe you tellin' the truth. This is very dangerous. It could easily happen to yo' family if you was Ralthus. We got a group that just waitin' on something like that." An' he bust out and just went to cryin'—grown man, said he had been offered twelve hundred dollars. They was gonna give him six in advance; then after he do it, he would get the other six.

"But I ain't gonna. . . ."

I say, "We know you ain't gonna do it. We know one thang, if you do do it, you'a never live to see nothing, enjoy nothing. You go back an' tell them come to us, we waitin' on them."

I think he did go back, an' he scared his bossman; tell him we had a meetin' wit' him. He worked on out that year, and he move 'way from here up there on the other side of Greenwood [laughs]. He was afraid to live down here; everybody was treatin' him all right, but he didn't own no land down here.

It don't pay nobody to try to be bad. It don't pay nobody to be too afraid. You must remember, a white man ain't nothing but a meat man just like me, you, and everybody else, and if he find out that you can look him in his eyes and are not afraid of him, he ain't gonna do nothing. My daddy told me always stop and git a understanding what somebody sayin' to you. Look a man ret in the eye and let him know you a man just like he is.

What do you think would happen to people that went to register to vote and wanted to borrow some money from the bank? What would happen to 'em?

SD: The biggest portion of 'em would get turned down for the money.

Did you know of anyone that got turned down?

SD: I known some who were keeping civil rights workers at their homes during that time. They had students from Yale University, Harvard University, different colleges, would come in here in the summer time an' teach peoples about registerin' and what did it mean, and about voting. An' I've heard of those they was stayin' with goin' to the bank to borrow some money, and the man would aks them, "What do you wanna borrow some money for? To feed them hungry civil rights workers you got with you?"

An' then you had Ku Klux Klans who was ridin' at night tryin' to scare people. You take Mileston—over there at the sanctified church right 'cross the railroad there at Mileston was where the first meetings was held in the county. The meetings got to be so big and so important that they built what they call Holmes County Community Center. An' every third Sunday they would hold a county-wide meeting. Then the Movement started in different areas, like Durant had a place, Ebenezer had a place, Lexington, Mount Olive, and other smaller places. But then everybody was comin' together that third Sunday to have a meeting. An' then they finally opened up an office in Lexington which they called the FDP—Freedom Democratic Party. And you had a chairman of the FDP and board of directors for the whole county.

Did you ever participate in Freedom Summer?

SD: I participated. They had workshops and whatnots all over the county during the summer.

Can you recall some of the freedom schools we had in Holmes County?

SD: Well, one was located at Mileston, the other one was located out there at Sunny Mount, Mount Olive, out there at West—Pilgrim Rest.

Were there mostly blacks teaching or whites teaching?

SD: It was a mix. We had a white couple who came here during the time they were building that center, had stayed for five years—Henry Lorenzi an' his wife was named Sue Lorenzi. Well, Henry's dead. They had a house over in Lexington after they left here; worked at the civil rights house there in Pecan Grove. They was too nice, a young couple, but they help out a whole lot. Henry was a smart man, but he always stayed in the background. He'd let some black do whatever he or she was able to do. Henry never did have no trouble out of these whites; they was half afraid of him.

Some of those civil rights workers was senators' sons and daughters or congressmen's sons and daughters; some were lawyers' sons and daughters. They would come into Holmes County and all over the state and would sit with blacks, they would ride with blacks; people even stayed in black people's houses. They may stay with the poorest of blacks that didn't even have a chair for them to sit in. Some people way back then were sitting on blocks of wood in their house for a chair. Or a fifty-pound lard can. Like they'd come in here and sit down on this floor.

I think they were drilled by SNCC before they ever came here. That the only way they were gon' get these people to believe in them or go and register. Come here and stay with us and prove to us that they wadn't no more than us, and it wasn't right for us saying no "Yes ma'am" or "No ma'am" or "Yes sir" to 'em. Say yes and no. They tol' us that. An' they [the white civil rights workers] done a good job with gettin' it across to us.

Did any of the civil rights workers ever stay in your house or your friends' or neighbors' house?

SD: Lot of 'em stayed in my friend and neighbors' houses. I kept Abe, the man that built that community center, came from California. I kept him the first night that he came to Mississippi. Yes, I kept civil rights workers; I've kept high as five at one time. Doctors—they were in here lookin' at the situation, seein' how was thangs. Yes, after we start keepin' 'em down there at Mileston, they went to staying all out there round Mount Olive. Mr. Taft Bailey kept a lot of 'em and all out there at West. Just about all over the county, but more of 'em stayed around Mileston 'cause this where the Movement started—down here.

How did Abe adjust to the Southern culture?

SD: Oh, Abe was one hundred percent adjusted. He was a carpenter; he built that center, and he raised the money. Ya know, he knew people that was rich, and he just called 'em on the telephone and say, "I need ten thousand dollars." In a day or two, that money was here, cashier check. They go up there to the bank, and they didn't wanna take it 'cause they know he was buildin' that center down there where black people—and white—would have somewhere to meet at. And even after it got built, Abe stayed on round here for a good while. Abe really liked it here. Abe don't care nothing 'bout no money, I tell you that. He say long as he helpin' somebody that he feel like need help, he say he gits all the joy in the world out of that.

Were some of these civil rights workers that come from the North scared when they came down here?

SD: It was quite a few of 'em from the North got arrested. But they was just raised in a different attitude; they just wadn't afraid. I know we had a lawyer [Mel Leventhal] came here and stopped at a service station in Durant, and they bust all the lights out of his car where he couldn't even see out. He had to call for someone to come get him at the service station. He just went there 'n' when they found out who he was, bam! Back, front, park lights and all, sho' did.

Marian Wright was a black attorney down in Jackson, and she was the one that integrated all the schools in the state of Mississippi. It was 'bout eight or nine lawyers workin' wit' her. Mel was working on her staff, but he lived here in Holmes County, working wit' us. He was in charge of this school integration in the full.

Marian Wright open this Civil Rights Movement, and she was a smart lady—wadn't that large, but she knowed what she was about. I went to Washington with her on a plane, my first time going. Now she opened doors there and tol' people what was happenin' in Mississippi. Some nights til one and two o'clock, havin' people comin' to our rooms, aksin' us questions like y'all doin' ret now. And we tol' 'em that people was choppin' cotton for two or three dollars a day, ten hours a day. They just couldn't believe it no kinda way. They say, "None of us been havin' peoples come up here and tell nothin'. . . ."

I say, "Well, you ain't got to take our word."

Say, "We believe y'all."

"You come down there, you'll see." And they beginnin' to sendin' peoples in here, to investigate what was goin' on. And that's what brought about that big change.

We had had a Head Start that they call CDGM [Child Development Group of Mississippi]. This Head Start first opened at Mileston, Mount Olive, Old Pilgrim Rest, Second Pilgrim Rest. Out there at Saints had it, and then later they got it at Ambrose. But anyhow that thang was branging' too many poor peoples together. That's the first thang that started to wakin' up peoples. All over they was having workshops. People was meetin' people from other counties. CDGM was over 'bout twenty-four counties, thirty; bunch of counties in the state of Mississippi. It was the biggest thang going for poor people. These white folk got together and come up wit' what they call a "CAP" program [Community Action Program], do away wit' CDGM. That's how Central Mississippi come about wit' a six-county outfit.

Did any civil rights people, local Movement people, get jobs in these programs with Central Mississippi Incorporated (CMI) or Head Start?

SD: We had quite a few right here in Mileston that was in the Civil Rights Movement all the way 'til they got a job with CMI. And some

The Holmes County Community Center was built in Mileston in 1964 to serve as a base for the local Movement. In addition to meetings and social events, the Center housed a child-care program before Head Start came into existence. Pictured here is worker Rosie Head in the Center kitchen area in summer 1965 when Head Start funds became available. Ms. Head remains the head teacher at the Mileston Head Start in 1991.

of 'em is yet working with the CMI. You take like Rosie Head over there at Mileston and Dessie Smith and Elease Gallion workin' and still workin' with Central Mississippi. The Head Start program helped many persons had worked in it get homes, and also help them school-age children. I know quite a few; they got children went all the way through college. And they wouldn't a made it if they hadn't been workin' there, where they had some financial help.

What do you think still needs to be done?

SD: My suggestion is we've accomplished some thangs. It took a long time 'fore a black person come able to win an election. Representative Robert Clark won out in 1967. An' that was just amazing 'cause he ran against a real big money man and beat him. An' then they said they wadn't gon' let him be seated down there at the House, but he was seated.

It's a lot of people now livin' in nice brick homes ya never woulda got then. A lot of peoples are bein' paid; they got good jobs. But the big, real top-paying jobs—blacks still being left out. Now, 'less I'm badly fooled, ain't no white gonna ever soon be she'ff no more. And you see we got a black superintendent of education, black tax assessors, black supervisors, black she'ff. Course, some of 'em ain't up to the part like they should be. But ain't none of them thangs woulda happened.

Now, it's a whole lot more that coulda been done if black people had stuck together like they was together then. It's a whole lot more we coulda been done. But the white man went to givin' 'em jobs, tellin' 'em how good they doin'. They started makin' a lil' money and went to thinkin' only about theyselves. You ain't gon' build no Movement with folk thinkin' about they own selves.

MRS. BEE JENKINS

"Ready to Shoot Lead"

KENNETH SALLIS & LEKESHIA BROOKS

Mrs. Bee Jenkins is an elderly woman who, at first sight, reminds you of your grandmother. She wears butterfly glasses and is short, chubby, and always smiling. She has shoulder-length hair with bits of gray that she usually wears loose. But behind this sweet woman of such warmth lies an activist of extraordinary courage, commitment, and wisdom.

Mrs. Bee Jenkins played an important role in the Movement here in Holmes County. For example, she has helped plan and participated in many marches. She first became a part of the Movement while she lived in Durant. She helped integrate the hospital, the cafés, and the train station. She said that when they integrated the train station, the white people wouldn't even come into the station. They stood outside in the cold waiting for the train.

Today, Mrs. Jenkins still participates in the Movement. She was a named plaintiff in a 1985 lawsuit against the City of Lexington. When others dropped their names from the lawsuit because of pressure from local white citizens, Mrs. Bee stood strong. Because of the courage she and others displayed, we now have black elected officials here in Lexington for the first time in 154 years. Wherever you find injustice in Holmes County, you can still find Mrs. Bee standing up for the rights of others.

[In the following interview, the speakers are Mrs. Bee Jenkins (**BJ**) and a crew from Mississippi Educational Television (**TV**) who filmed the interview.]

Tell us about your involvement in the Movement.

BJ: I got peoples to redish [register] to vote. I would carry them up to the courthouse, and they would redish to vote. I would just take 'em up to the circuit clerk office. Henry B. McClellan at that time was the circuit clerk. They would write they names, they addresses, they ages, and all. And then they become registered to vote.

Was there any problems when you were taking the people up there with Henry McClellan?

BJ: Not at the time when I took 'em up there. But beforehand, when I was registered to vote, I wadn't able to register at the courthouse. I had to register under the post office with the registrars. So many like Mr. Hartman Turnbow, Mr. Warren G. Booker, Reverend Whittaker, Reverend Russell, and many more—they had a very hard time. They would sic the dogs on them and try to run 'em away. But they never did give up. They would go back every day and try to get registered.

Why was it that you had to be registered at the post office instead of the courthouse?

BJ: They didn't allow you to redish to vote. They would ask so many questions. And I had a job. I had to be back at work a certain time. It made it so inconvenient for the black peoples to register. So they sent the federal registrars to Mississippi. They would help the peoples to register to vote.

Mr. McClellan didn't register you? Who registered you?

BJ: The registrars in from Washington. It was easy for me to get registered there because it didn't take long, and so I would be able to go back to my job on time.

Were there many people afraid to register because of the risks?

BJ: Yes, many, many was afraid to redish.

Why wasn't you afraid?

BJ: I never have been afraid of white people. The funny thing about it, I was workin' for a doctor, and I was a very strong worker then in the Movement. One day he told me, "Bee, you be going somewhere at night. I don't know where, but I think you be going out there with them freedom riders." Which I did.

I said, "Well, you can't say." That's all I would tell him. My parents didn't teach me to be afraid. We all was just different colors, but we all was human beings. And we were all God's children.

Did your husband support you or help participate?

BJ: Yes, he did, and if he didn't, I was going on anyway. 'Cause I was determined to see blacks have better opportunity. I just grew up with that in me. My grandparents and all would tell me how they ended up doing, and it just really bothered me. I said if the Lord's willin', I'm gonna do something about makin' a change in this community.

What were some of the tactics that you used to get other people registered who were afraid?

BJ: I would go in their home and sit down and talk with them and ask them if they wanted to register so they'd be able to vote. Or I'd meet 'em on the street. They'd say, yes, they did, but they was afraid. I'd say, "Well, nothing to be afraid of. You not a citizen of Mississippi until we are registered to vote." And I would convince them that they didn't have anything to fear. Some of 'em was afraid to go up there alone. I said, "I'm a little old short lady. You wouldn't be afraid with me. I'll go with you."

Did anything ever happen to these people because they registered to vote?

BJ: No, it wadn't any violence at that time, after they had sent peoples to help black peoples to register. Before, they would ask 'em all kind of questions because they didn't want 'em to be able to register.

They would ask these questions on literacy tests?

BJ: Yes, they would stand and ask 'em, face to face, 'bout how many bubbles in a bar of soap or other unnecessary questions.

Did many people get registered?

BJ: Yes, after they sent a lot of these registrars in here to help the black peoples to register. When they left, they passed a law that Henry McClellan, the registrar, must register blacks. That must be. And so he did. And after he found out that black peoples was goin' to get registered, who but him comes walkin' up to my door one day when his term was out. He asked me to vote for him. I said "Well, I sure ain't gonna miss voting!" I left him like that. You don't tell them anything.

After the peoples in the hills got registered, we had problems trying to get the people from the Delta to register. A lot of those people lived on plantations and worked from sun to sun. On the plantation, they had these little houses that was built in the back of they bossman house. And the road you had to pass to go to they house would go right by his house. And so lots of 'em was afraid for you to come in to get them registered to vote. They knowed if the bossman found out they was goin' to redish or somebody was coming to take him up there to register, they would beat them and wadn't merciful.

So we would have meetings at churches and different homes. We decided that we would slip onto the plantation at daybreak. You always had somebody to let the people know you was gonna slip them out. The next morning it would be a field of us, while they would take the peoples that lived on the place to get redished. We worked in they place, and they slipped off so they could register.

The bossman didn't recognize you?

BJ: No, he didn't recognize any of us. All he wanted was a field full of folks.

If you'd got caught, what do you think would've happened?

BJ: Well, I didn't think about that. Because we was really sincere in what we was doing. We knowed we wanted those people to be registered so that we would be able to put some black peoples in the positions that they was holding. We knew that if we didn't get them to register, we wouldn't be able to get anybody elected to different positions, like Representative Robert Clark.

Now we have supervisors and a superintendent; we have black peoples working in the bank. Before, we didn't have any of that. We didn't have good-paying jobs. Only jobs that black peoples would have was maid and yardboys. After we got peoples to redish to vote, then we had problems still.

They had water fountains like in the courthouse. It would be in writing, big letters: one for the "white" and one for the "colored."

And in these cafés, black peoples couldn't go inside to sit down and eat. They had to have a little window that you go to order your food. They would shove your food out to you through that window. And so we didn't think that was right. I and a lady went to the Ritz Café in Durant one time. She said "Beatrice, let's go get us a sandwich." I thought you could go inside and sit down and eat, 'cause I hadn't been long moved down here. And she went round to the kitchen where the cooks was.

I said, "We supposed to go through the front door." She said, "*No, that's whites!*" I said, "No, this is the wrong place for me." I didn't buy a sandwich. I backed out. It was so many places closed to the blacks. The Dairy Bar in Durant had two windows—"white" was on one side and "colored" on the other. A group of us went to the "white" to be served.

"Y'all go to the next window there where it say 'colored.'" You'd just stand there. If she didn't serve you, you just go away. If they did serve you a drink or whatever, they'd just fill it up with salt. It would be so salty when you take the first drink, you would have to spit it out. That's the way they'd do at some of those restaurants: They would serve your food so salty you couldn't eat it, and you had to pay for it.

How did you go about integrating hospitals?

BJ: We went to the hospital, and they had separate places for the black and the white. But black folks were being admitted to the hospital just like the whites and had to pay just as much. So we sat down in the white waiting room. We wadn't gonna take no for an answer. We just kept on going back there and sitting down.

What did the whites do when you came over to their side?

BJ: They would look at you funny and hard. They wouldn't come on out with anything, but they'd just get up and mumble and turn real red. You could see it in their face that they didn't like it.

Did the receptionist say anything to you?

BJ: Oh yes, they'd say: "This where you supposed to be sittin', not over here!" But you wouldn't move. And at the railroad station, they had separate black waiting rooms. So they decided they would integrate that. So they did. The blacks started to going over and sitting on the white [side], and they didn't like that. The ticket agent would say, "You're in the wrong place. Blacks are down there." The whites stopped coming and sitting in they sitting room. They didn't come in the railroad station. They'd buy their ticket and walk back out. The blacks is the only one will still sit there.

Would people ever be harassed or attacked on their way to the train station because of that?

BJ: Some of 'em attempted to hit ya. But they was afraid 'cause we was all in groups, mens and women, maybe three or four. They couldn't handle all of us, because somebody might have some lead to put in 'em, and they didn't want that. They just walk beside you and call you "niggers" and everything. And sometimes 'tend they had a gun in they pocket. They might have. But we didn't let them stop us. I would get threatening letters left in my mailbox. They would tell what their and our foreparents were like, that this have been the tradition, and, "If y'all go on and let them civil rights peoples alone, we could still get along."

We just kept on going because we had a goal that we was trying to reach. If we was gonna spend our money with them, we thought we had a right to a decent place to sit down, too. The black washroom there was undecent, unsanitary. They never did clean it.

Then they didn't want to give people jobs, so that was another fight between the blacks and the whites. At first, they said they would hire blacks. They agreed to hire blacks and whites fifty/fifty. So they brought the factory in. Then they wouldn't hire any black people. So we had to go to Washington and talk with the senators, representatives, and all. Sat down and told 'em 'bout the situation in Holmes County, that they brought in the factories and still wouldn't hire any blacks.

Black people wadn't able to work in the welfare office. Black people didn't have a job at the doctor's office no more than with a broom. It was a mop and a broom job. They didn't have anybody hired in the bank, and the hospital was segregated. We started boycotting, and the senator and the congressman made it possible for the black peoples to be hired in the factories. When we got back down here, they had started to hiring the blacks fifty/fifty. To get peoples in these jobs, like the bank and the hospital and all, then we had to boycott.

After you boycotted all these places and finally got black peoples to be hired, were they treated equal?

BJ: No, they weren't treated as equals. They was treated unfair; they didn't treat 'em with courtesy.

Did that go on for a long time?

BJ: Oh yes. In fact, it could be better now. Blacks are being discriminated [against] until this date. We don't have equal opportunities as they does.

Besides boycotting these places, did you ever march against them?

BJ: Yes, I did. We were marching because they still hadn't hired any blacks in the stores as cashiers. They had the broom job and the mop job. A woman worked for twenty-five cents a week, all day long. Twenty-five cents, some ole clothes, maybe eggs and milk or something. It made my blood boil. I just couldn't understand why, because we had to go to the store and buy like they did. And we would go spend our money with those merchants. We had people qualified enough to be cashiers. We wadn't satisfied 'til we were able to get some black cashiers in those stores, in the banks, and all.

What happened in the marches?

BJ: Well, we would march and sing. That's one thing they didn't want us to do: march around the square, and sing and clap. They asked us not to. But we did. And after they see that we wadn't gonna stop singing, they put us in jail.

What happened while you were in jail?

BJ: We continued to sing. They asked us to hush, but we didn't. We continued to sing until that night. We had bondsmen; they would come and bond us out of jail.

These were people who didn't march with you but was still behind you in a way?

BJ: The people that bond us out didn't march. Because if they locked them up, there wouldn't be anybody to get us out. We had peoples just to make bonds, that was they job. Not to march, but to bond us out if we got in jail. And they had to be homeowners so they would be able to bond us out.

When you participated in marches, were you ever threatened?

BJ: Yes, in fact, we have had the Ku Klux Klan where we were marching. That day it was only two of us marching; the rest was marching in another part of town. So they came round to scare us away. They stopped in the middle of the street with these great hoods on, tall hats, and all those white robes. I just stopped marching and went to the car where they was an' told 'em, "Now look, I know who you are. I don't know you by name, not now, but I know you in the merchandise business here in Lexington. I want you to know today that I'm not afraid. You live once and you die once. If today's the day, I'm ready. I'm not afraid." And I said, "What you need is to go somewhere an' pull off those robes and go back in your store and try to make you some money." I know I never have been afraid. I'm not the type.

What did they do when you told them that?

BJ: They stood there and looked at me. And I stood right there and looked at them. I told them right there, I wadn't moving. I wadn't afraid.

What would the sheriff do when you were marching?

BJ: We didn't have a black sheriff. We had a white sheriff here, and 'course he and the city police arrested us. One time we had a boycott here in town, trying to get the peoples not to shop in these stores. They'd better not go in that store because if they do, we gonna take care of them. And we know if they would go in the stores, we wouldn't get our freedom, wouldn't be able to get blacks hired in those stores as cashiers.

Andrew Smith at that time was the high sheriff here, and he was a really mean high sheriff. He had law enforcements from different towns gonna stop us marching. The streets was full of law enforcement. We was all marching, and they all gathered on the streets. We just stopped right across the street from K & B store, across from the courthouse. We all stood there. And all the law enforcements standing there with their big guns. I was working that day. Where I worked at, the lady tol' me if she was I, she wouldn't march that day, "because somebody gon' get killed."

I didn't tell her no, I wadn't gon' march, and I didn't tell her yes. When I finished my work, I walked outta her house, looked up, said a prayer, and went and got in the marching. And the law enforcements 'n' highway patrol was all gathered up there—you name 'em, they was there. I wadn't afraid. Because I know I had somebody there who was on my side. And that was Jesus; he was able to take care of me. That who I depend on and put my trust in.

Did you ever have to to defend yourself while you was marching?

BJ: We had men to do that, because every day you get out there, it was really hot. Now I'm tellin' you, you had to be a strong person to get in that march because they had all those law enforcements. But we had black mens that wadn't afraid. They would stand between us. They would be on the lefthand side and we be on the righthand side next to the stores. They was well protected, too. They were ready to start a war, too. So it was really serious. We wadn't playing. We was spending our money in stores, and we thought we need some black people hired in those stores. You can't get a job done if you're afraid; you have to have courage to do that.

When you say the men were well protected, do you mean they had guns?

BJ: Oh yeah, they had fire. Ready to shoot lead! If they started anything, they was ready, too. They had guns.

I often heard that the Movement was really nonviolent. . . .

BJ: Dr. Martin Luther King said it was nonviolent. It was nonviolent until they brought in the law enforcements. After they came in with their guns, our menfolk thought we had to be protected, too. They didn't bother them unlessen they tried to start shooting at us or got violent with us.

Do you remember a time when some whites came by and shot at the church?

BJ: Yes, we met at Second Pilgrim Rest Church, north of Durant. It would be a churchfull every night. We would go to those meetings; we didn't care how it'd be rainin', snowin', sleetin'—we went. It got so bad out there: How they would ride the gravel road, started to burning crosses out there and shooting while we would be on the inside meetin', tryin' to transact business. So the black men would go buy them some high-powered rifles and started shooting at those cars. They took off and didn't come back out there.

Eventually we decided not to meet out there; we didn't want to get those people's church burned down. Then we would meet at houses in town. We'd move our meeting from place to place; then they wouldn't know. Mr. Grove was community chairman of Beat Two, and Mr. Howard Taft Bailey was our countywide chairman.

Were there many women involved in the Movement?

BJ: Oh yes! Mens, women, and children. Boys and girls.

Were the younger people ever tempted to use violence?

BJ: Yes, those kids wadn't afraid either. If anybody say something, they'll be ready to start a fight [laughs]. But we would always tell them, "No, no, no!" We'd stop 'em. 'Course I can understand them if you walking around, and they call you a "nigger" and lotta bad names. 'Cause I didn't like it either, and the young people's quick to get fired up. So we had to kind of talk to them, ask them to be nonviolent. Because we wouldn't get our rights if we were violent too. Somebody might be gettin' hurt, and we didn't want that.

What do you think Martin Luther King would have thought of y'all using violence?

BJ: He would always preach nonviolence. He didn't want it to be violent because he know that wadn't the way. If you want to be elected to these different offices, you had to be sincerely what you're doing with nonviolence. Because some was killed, some was beaten, some houses were bombed in this marching. It was a lot of violence on they side, the white side.

Do you remember the mayor of Durant, C. H. Blanton?

BJ: Yes, because he lives in Durant now and has a pressing shop there. He spoke up for the blacks; he said he didn't go along with burning crosses. And they burned a cross in his yard.

What was the biggest march y'all ever had, and what was its purpose?

BJ: We had so many. I tell you at that time we had a large number of peoples, 'bout four or five hundred peoples marching, and it may've been more. Blacks didn't have any jobs and wadn't able to support they family. Going to the Delta, they would pick 'n' chop cotton to help support their family. They didn't have jobs, wadn't working in the factory 'cause it wadn't many factories at that time. And everybody wanted a job, was concerned about being hired. We would have a meeting, gather maybe at churches, and plan whatever we wanted next. We didn't just come up on the streets and march.

Were there any blacks on the city council here in Lexington?

BJ: We never did have any on city council 'til two years ago. Only thang we did was pay our city taxes at the city hall. They was all white. Didn't have any black in city government to represent any blacks. We didn't even have a voice to make policy for the city because we wadn't allowed to participate in the meeting. We can come sit and be quiet, but we couldn't speak, 'cause we didn't have anybody there to represent us 'til we got two black aldermen elected. And we couldn't get them elected until we had to change the system.

How did the blacks you elected help you when they got in office?

BJ: They enable us to sit and make policies.

Do you think that there's still a movement going on today for the rights of black people?

BJ: Oh, yes. We have the ROCC and the Freedom Democratic Party. And we still having some problems with the whites. Here, about a couple of weeks ago, we had a black lady harassed by a policeman. They said that she called him a bad name. She and a friend was riding together, and he just pulled up to the yield sign by the time they did. She yield for him and was talking to a friend. He said that she was talking to him. They had her to pull aside and get out the car. And they harassed her and arrested her unfairly and took her to jail.

She had been in a serious car accident and had got her leg broken. It was so bad that they had put pins in her leg. Anyway, they forced her in back of the car against her will. See, she can't ride on a back seat of a car because she can't bend her knees. She have to ride on the front so she can keep her legs stretched out. By forcing her in that car, bending, pushing, and pulling on her leg, that moved some of those pins in her leg. And so now her leg is all swollen up from that harass from the police two weeks ago.

Would you sing us a freedom song?

BJ: Ohoooh freedom, ohoooh freedom,
Ohoooh freedom aft' a while, aft' a while.
And before I be a slave, I'll be buried in my grave,
And go home to my Father and be saved.
[She repeated the verse two more times.]

TV: How do you feel about being interviewed today?

BJ: I feel fine. I really does. Because that's what I fought for—our freedom.

TV: Do you think what you talked about today with these two students can help them, and why?

BJ: I hope so, because you can see the little gray hair in my head. You know that mean I'm getting older. We all fading out, away, and I don't know the day, neither the hour when the Lord gonna say, "It's enough. Come on home." And I would like to know that we'll be leaving something behind that will carry on the way we have started.

I'm so proud of these young peoples because I have always wanted young people to get involved so they could know the struggles we came through to get them where they are today. Some lost their lives, too. And so I'm just really happy. I'm glad someone is eventually gonna write a book about Holmes County, because it's been a need so long. I really feel like shouting just to know these young peoples really interested in the Movement and to carry on after we have gone on to glory.

MR. T. C. JOHNSON

The Dirt Farmers Started the Movement

REGINALD SKINNER & JACKIE COLLINS

Mr. T. C. Johnson stands about five feet ten inches tall. He has skin the color of coffee ice cream. Mr. Johnson has dark curly hair with salt and pepper sideburns and a light moustache. A cowboy hat sits on top of his head like a cherry on ice cream. He loves that hat because he's worn it about the last ten years. It does look good on him.

His large yard is covered with a carpet of thick green grass. He also has a trampoline for his grandchildren who live next door. His yard is full of dogs and cats. Cows graze in his pasture out back, and pigs wallow in their muddy pen. Trees give plenty of shade. One big oak tree sits right in front of his house, and I mean big.

Mr. T. C. lives in a four-bedroom, white house with a tin top and black trimming. He invited us into his living room. The first thing I noticed was a wooden sculpture of a black clenched fist that his son had bought.

Mr. Johnson is a polite man. He offered us breakfast before we got started. During the interview he spoke loudly and clearly and explained things well. Sometimes he would waggle his finger to emphasize a point. He looked at us as he explained to make sure we understood. Just before we got started, he drank half a cup of coffee, but he was so into the interview that he forgot about his coffee until it was cold.

Mr. T. C. Johnson was one of the first to get involved in the Civil Rights Movement in the Lexington area. He sent his children to the white school and ran for the county Board of Supervisors on the Freedom Democratic Party slate in 1967. He didn't win, but one FDP candidate did. Robert Clark, a school teacher and basketball coach, was elected as the first black to sit in the Mississippi state legislature since Reconstruction.

Mr. Johnson tells about the trials and tribulations he and other activists had to endure during the '60s. He goes on to talk about Eddie Noel, the sharpshooting black man who killed three white Holmes Countians in 1954.

144

[In the following interview, **TC** is Mr. T. C. Johnson.]

Mr. Johnson, how did you first get involved with the Civil Rights Movement?

TC: When I first got in the Movement, they had me like a so-called leader to encourage others to come to meetings because a lot of people knew me. I had seen a lot of abuse, and this made me make an effort to better conditions in Holmes County.

What happened when you first tried to register to vote?

TC: When I first went to try register to vote, it was only three of us— Ed [McGaw] Jr. and Old Man [Lucas] Sims and myself. We were met by some German Shepherds and the sheriff, Andrew P. Smith, and some of the deputies. This kinda put a little fear in your mind. Old Man Sims (who was practically blind) was in front, and the dogs was just charging at his legs, but he couldn't see. We still had the courage to proceed into the courthouse.

We had to go to the circuit clerk's office to fill out forms. It was what grade you were, how old, were you a citizen, and a whole lotta questions. That was under Henry B. McClellan.

We stayed in there so long 'til I was leanin' up on the counter, and he asked me did I wanna go to jail. And I said, "No, the only thing we came up here for is to try register to vote." And he asked me if I wanted to see the sheriff. I told him, "No, I didn't come to see the sheriff."

Then he messed around. We was in there from 'bout nine o'clock 'til 'bout two. He would go get coffee, and it would take him 'bout two hours and a half to return. That's how slow and unconcerned they were about you trying to get registered to vote.

How many times did you try?

TC: Several times. The next time, a pretty good bunch was going, and me and my wife and two more ladies went up. They were still giving you the runaround, askin' you all kind of silly questions. It was still dragging feet and wastin' time, and only one or two could get in that day.

They would treat you very ugly, talking about throwing you in jail and calling the sheriff. It was awful, and you couldn't get a lotta peoples to even go up because they was already fearful. They knew that white folk was running the county, and if you didn't do what they wanted, they would make it hard for ya. Or catch you on the road and beat you up. And wasn't nothing did about it, because they wasn't handling whites for doing anything to blacks.

But after I went, it gave me courage to go back where I'd be a registered voter. And that'd make me proud. We were the first three from the east side of Lexington 'cause there were a group ahead of us from Mileston, the first fourteen. They took a lotta abuse. I think Smith cursed 'em out and made 'em get off the grass.

What do ya think the sheriff's main reason was for being at the courthouse at this time?

TC: His purpose was to disencourage blacks from coming. He could get you upset and afraid. Lotta people just wouldn't go if they saw the dogs out there. They would be saying things to you, "Get the hell offa that grass." They had signs out there: "Keep off the grass." If you step on the grass, they would carry you to jail.

Were you ever threatened for trying to register to vote?

TC: Not at that time. It came down later when we started entering children in the white schools. And I put my youngest son Leander Johnson over there and they cut my funds off—what I was borrowing to farm on. They came and told me a group was comin' to see was I being paid by the government. I told 'em I just wanted my child to get a good education so he'd be able to make it through the world.

When you sent your son to the public school, where did the blacks go to school before then if they didn't go to the white public schools?

TC: They were going to Ambrose High down in the Schoolhouse Bottom. Dr. Mallory had Saints Academy, a sanctified school. Now, you could go there and pay or go to Ambrose. But they [the whites] didn't want you interfering into "their" schools. When he left Ambrose, I sent him to LES [Lexington Elementary School], which was the so-called white school.

That morning, when we were going to register [the children in the school], you had your bankers, your lawyers, all your top white business peoples standing on the sidewalk pointin' you out. They would cut your trade, stop your credit on clothes or groceries at stores—they would have you singled out.

But I was determined to stick, to break this segregation thing if it wasn't no more than eight or ten got to keep their children there. Things worked on out; they got in the school.

But they would fight 'em or scare 'em through the school hours; even made some of 'em jump out of the windows. They called me to come check on my son because he didn't have the ability. Better if I would take him out and let him work on the farm or give him some kinda skill, like fixing on car motors. Several times I caught him—they would have him out in the hall standing up on one leg or something like that.

What type of experience did your son get from going?

TC: He was 'fraid sometimes because they would hit him, have his lip bleeding. But I would give him the courage to keep going: "You'll have to take a few punches. This help you to grow and learn. Now, you get your education; you'll get through the world much better. They ain't gonna do too much, or I'll be over there." So he went through that year.

The next year they would only let first and second grade go. I had my other daughter Sylvia and Bubba go, and he would have somebody there to look after. That made him feel better. So Sylvia and Bubba graduated from over there.

Were the hospital and doctors' offices segregated at this time?

TC: Yes, all the doctors' offices—you had white and black. They wouldn't use "black" then. They would use "colored" and "negro." You wouldn't be able to go in the front; you had to go mostly in the side. The hospital, too, had a ward down there for just blacks.

Once I did carry a group of six or eight guys up in this white café north of Lexington; they got a liquor store there now. We was going about a couple of hours before the usual closing time. And when I parked and they start going toward the door, I guess they saw 'em coming. We didn't get a chance to sit down and order. They didn't tell us we couldn't come and sit down; they had another method of getting us out, by putting water down and mopping the floors.

What was the relationship between the young blacks in SNCC like Sam Block, Bob Moses, and Hollis Watkins and the local activists?

TC: They came in to help black peoples get courage to try register to vote, to help us get peoples organized. SNCC and CORE was first and was kinda like the freedom riders coming down South. They had a staff and connections with lawyers from the North, and they would come down and help us do sit-ins and go into places where blacks wadn't allowed. They could come in and mingle pretty good. They knew partly what they were doing. They could get more of the people together at these meetings than we who were living here.

Why was that?

TC: I guess the people were just really searching for good leadership and somebody to stand up and tell 'em what the whites couldn't do to 'em. Because the blacks here were slow about moving. But they [the SNCC and CORE workers] would come with us and get peoples to promise to come out and help.

How did the white volunteers that came down during freedom summer get on with everybody?

TC: They would fall in and fit right on in. When they would talk, lot of 'em would agree 'long with 'em. You'd have a few say, "I ain't gon' fool with that mess." But you would get over half of 'em to cooperate with ya but be shaky and fearful. They were coming from the North and kinda had a little more hang with 'em than some of the blacks here. Some of 'em came six months, a year, and left. But Sue and Henry Lorenzi stayed on throughout the whole action because, when they left, most blacks what wanted to register had done been up and registered.

Explain to us about the Mississippi Freedom Democratic Party.

TC: That was a party to help get peoples registered to vote. And it would help you get organized to go sit in a lotta these places and to try to break segregation. It was formed in 1964 'cause blacks wasn't allowed in the regular Democratic Party. By 1967 we had enough blacks registered in Holmes County so the FDP ran a group of candidates.

And you ran for supervisor with the FDP in 1967. Why did you run?

TC: To make better conditions in the county. A lotta places they didn't even drag any gravel. That service was only rendered to some whites. Occasionally blacks would get it because you was a "yes man." Now, if you play that game, the man would give you a lotta rocks and fix yours like everybody else. But I was always a man that stood up for what I thought was right, and sometimes it makes you be the last one to receive any benefits.

Blacks were left out of most positions. Everything you went to—if you went before the judge, ya goin' 'fore a white judge. If you went 'fore the sheriff, you goin' with all white in there, and you bein' mistreated in jail. If you went before the polices in town, ya going against all whites. So blacks had just 'bout's much chance as a rabbit. 'Cause they had groups that would come and hang and shoot 'em. Wouldn't be anything did if he was black, if a white man did it. Now if a black man did it, they would find him, if they had to get the National Guard.

What other blacks were running for what other positions?

TC: Some was going for constable, justice court judge, chancery clerk, and tax assessor. We were practically running for all the positions. At this time a lotta teachers came out and joined us at the grassroots level, after it got wide open, while they was not afraid of losing their jobs.

Where did you get the money to pay for this?

TC: I mostly paid out of my pocket, because I always had land, a few cattle and hogs. And my daddy owned quite a bit a land came down to me. I bought about sixty acres of my own after I came in possession of it. So I was able to do almost what I wanted. Only I wasn't able to get enough votes to win that supervisor position.

Did they try to keep blacks from voting?

TC: Of course. That was the first priority. Then they could always get who they wanted to.

What did you do on voting day?

TC: I would go to each polling place, shake hands with people, try to gain more support, and check out was it being fair and square. 'Cause we had federal observers, but they would just sit 'round; didn't seem like they were much help. When some problems arise, don't seem like they would take any action 'til it was over. And that would be late because when the other candidate won, that was it for the next four years.

Were there any kinda disturbances on voting day?

TC: Yes, we'd have quite a few. White and blacks would kinda get uptight. I remember once when we were down to Mileston, this white man came in and wanted to stop the election. We was tryin' to get in touch with Representative Clark to see if we could call in federal observers on him, because they had the peoples afraid.

Why do you think Robert Clark won, but you and all the other FDP candidates lost?

TC: That's just politics they played. They had two chances to one of outwinning the blacks because our peoples can be easy persuaded. They [white candidates] would come to our churches and give money to some of the top leaders who would get up and announce their name: "Ooh, Mr. So and So gave so much." We wasn't able to go to their churches or to where they were gathering. We always had our doors open for them. The whites told us, "Well, y'all got one, and ya should be satisified." But we wants what we deserve, we don't wanna just stop at one.

Who would you say first started the Movement?

TC: I'd say it's mostly the farmers—the poor farmers, the dirt farmers.

What advantage did they have more than the other people for beginning the Movement?

TC: Well, some of the farmers had a acre or two, or ten or twenty, so he had his own little shack and farm; he was making his living mostly from the earth. The teachers had to go through the school 'sociation, and they were always afraid that if they got out there, the superintendent and the rest of the people would get on 'em; and if they didn't quit, they would fire 'em.

But now we did get one teacher—Mrs. Bernice Montgomery. She was the first teacher that came out and really stuck with the Movement. Seem like she had her mind made up. And her husband saw the Movement

Robert G. Clark (candidate for state representative), Mary Lee Hightower (candidate for circuit clerk), and Burrell Tate (Beat 3 FDP leader) are part of an FDP campaign caravan in October 1967. Schoolteacher Clark won and became the first black since Reconstruction to sit in the Mississippi legislature, a post he holds in 1991. Ms. Hightower was defeated by a narrow margin in the 1967 election, and the other FDP candidates for major office also lost. Still, Mr. Clark's election was a stunning victory for the Movement.

needed help so he got in it, and that gave her more courage. She didn't care what happened back there at the job. She just came with a full desire to help the people move forward.

What was the school board made up of, black or white?

TC: Ooh, it was white, all white. And the superintendent was white. So the teachers was really afraid to get out there. They wasn't gonna do anything and lose that check.

Was there any tension between the poor farmers who were first involved in the Civil Rights Movement and the teachers and preachers who came in later on?

TC: Well, they were all tryin' to work toward one cause, but it would be a little tension because the grassroot people were the first to do anything, where the preachers and the teachers was afraid; they didn't wanna be involved at that time. So it was just the grassroot level people. And some of these old peoples didn't want you to talk about it or come to see you because they knew what would happen.

So it took the peoples with a lot of courage and the youngsters. Wherever there's a black church, we might could go there; but some of the preachers wouldn't let 'em invite us there. We got turned down a lot of times from the black minister. And black people were supporting him, paying him. He said he didn't believe in mixing politics with the Bible, but it was fear. He mostly was afraid because they whooped a few of 'em and bombed a few churches. The preacher didn't want his church burned down, and them old members was right along in his corner.

When they drove Reverend Trent out of town when he joined the first fourteen to register, did that example affect a lot of the preachers?

TC: That stopped a lot of the preachers. Reverend Russell was the top preacher that stuck in there from start to finish. These other preachers, they'd come in and hoop and holler well after everybody had registered and was runnin' for positions.

The whites couldn't do anything to you farmers?

TC: When you go to borrow money for farming, they'd tell you they kinda out, an' you could get it in July or August. By then everybody done already made the crop. You can't make nothin'; everybody done laid by. The stuff is growing, getting ready to start popping open.

I ran out of money an' needed to borrow some, an' that's the way I were treated. You leave one bank and go to apply to another bank. They would make a telephone call; when you get there, they already know you was on your way, and so you could get it if you come back in June or July.

What about FmHA [Farmers' Home Administration]? Were they the same?

TC: The FmHA was the same; they turned me down, too. After all the rest had turned me down, this new guy from Atlanta was down here. It was me and this other white guy in the office. He went in first and got eighteen thousand dollars with no collaterals. So he wrote him up.

And then he called me in. I said, "You wasn't here last week when I came in. But I wanna borrow a little money. I need about nine thousand. I's gonna put up two tractors and two hundred acres of land."

And he say, "Well, you could borrow eighteen or twenty thousand if you wanted to."

I say I think the nine thousand will do.

He say, "Well, you can get it an' put it in any bank here if you want to."

I say, "Well, I got my wife up here doin' a lit' shopping. I'll go tell her. But first, are you right sure I can get this money?" I asked him three times.

He say, "Hell, I told you. I'm the appraiser. If I go out there and appraise your land and say it's worth thirty thousand, you can borrow thirty thousand dollars. But first, do anybody have a lien on your land?"

I say, "No sir."

He say, "Where you borrow money from?"

I said from Holmes County Bank.

And he said, "I'm gonna go check your acres, and go to the courthouse to see is anybody got a lien on your land. And I'm goin' to Holmes County Bank where you borrowed that money from. I'll be on out to your house in twenty minutes."

It didn't take him more than fifteen minutes. I got in the truck and showed him my bottom land. Then he say, "Well, you can get out, Thomas. I'm sorry. You got too many woods on your land."

I say, "Hell, have you ever seen a place where you got over three hundred acres didn't have woods on there?"

He say, "I'm sorry."

I say, "I am too."

And he pulled off. I guess when he went by Holmes County Bank, them white folk told him I been helping the Movement and had put my son over there in the school. They say, "We got the rope around his neck and we chokin' him, so don't let him have it. We wanna put the squeeze on him."

Were other people active in the Movement done that way?

TC: A lot of them was threatened that they weren't gonna be able to get money. If they were on plantations, they'd have to up and move. So a lot of them would just pull on back 'cause you'd get harassed. If you own your own lit' shack, you were kinda free to take your own chances. So I was just taking my own chances.

If a white harassed you, were you ever tempted to use violence?

TC: I was fortunate that I didn't never arrive to that situation. But it happened to a lot of my friends.

Could you recall any particular situations?

TC: Hartman Turnbow, when they bombed his house and opened fire on him and his family in the Delta. He fired back. He opened fire on them, and this is what dispersed them, 'cause they can't stand when a black man go to throwing fire at a white man. They always been the ones that throwed the fire and you ran. But when you stop and return the fire, they moves; they'd leave you alone then and say you's crazy or you need treatment.

And John Malone down off from Ebenezer way. We left the church that Sunday, and when he got home, they parked outta the road. He had a car porch onto his house, and they shot all of his car glasses out, shot into his walls, tryin' to get him where he'd be afraid, wouldn't 'tend other meetings and things.

'Course the bullets could hit your childrens, your wife, you, or somebody get killed. Still, when they investigate, nothing be done. They'd say they could't find no trace. This would intimidate some blacks. Some would stop, just wouldn't assist you in no kind of help—financially or togetherness.

This was a dangerous game to be playing at that time. But it never made me wanna back away.

The importantest part is meeting together to give us a better understanding how to go about things. We wouldn't have it in the open where they could understand what we were gonna do; we would try to keep it a secret. Some would send some black in there to bring back the messages. And it would get back to the whites just about time we get through with the meeting.

So they were going back that quick 'n' tellin' 'em?

TC: Yeah, they'd know where the meetings are. You'd see patrolmens and the sheriff and constables riding around there. If we were gon' go march, they'd be knowing already before we go up.

Once I was coming from a meetin' down to Mileston; I had four or five youngsters with me. The sheriff and constables and game wardens would get across the track and catch us. I knew the country roads and the hills, so I could bring them a different route. Once, when we got back to Lexington, they had two cars across the blacktop. I just whirled and went the other way. Fear is part of it, but I was trying to shun trouble at that time.

Did you own your own weapon?

TC: Yes, we had little Saturday night specials that we'd hide; you couldn't let 'em be caught on you. You would have them in a place where you could get 'em if somebody intrude. A lot of the blacks was gettin' guns. We were packin' up stuff, so if there was just an all-out war, you'd have something to protect yourself with.

Did y'all have any disagreement about whether to use violence if necessary?

TC: Yes, a lot of 'em say they'd wanna carry different Saturday night specials in their pocket. But if you'd been searched, you'd be carried to jail; you was gonna have to pay the fine. And this would just further throw us back. That's when we would rather go nonviolence, and if they beat up anybody, you could get the Justice Department to help.

Did you feel your family might suffer?

TC: I were into it pretty deep. And it did make 'em suffer some. It'd hurt right then, but in the end it would be rewarded ya. Now, John Malone 'n' them and Cooper Howard, they had disaster in theirs, and some of their families got hurt. That hurt me, too. We would try to aid each other because we was in that same situation.

And when the whites was telling me they was gonna come give me a visit, this would make you get set up for the situation. So she [looking at his wife, Tine] would sleep in the early part of the night, and I would sleep after it get real late—one or two in the morning. Because it was a serious thing. If you got hurt or killed, you was just a dead man.

Did your wife ever have to use a weapon?

TC: No, I would sit the weapons up where she could get 'em in case somebody came up while I was gone. But it's fortunate she didn't never have to use 'em.

Could you tell us a little about Eddie Noel?

TC: Yes, he lived about two miles across from here on the Brozville road. He was a nice person. I didn't knowed him to misuse nobody. He had his fun—he believed in sippin' a little brew what they was making then out in the woods. Finally, he would sell a bit, would make ends meet for his household.

He was a fairly young man; he had been to the army and had served his country. Was a pretty good target shooter. I'd seen him go to fairs and shoot those little rifles and win 'til the man would tell him, "You can't shoot no more. Stand back! Let somebody else have it!"

They had a lil' ole honky-tonk joint down there in Ebenezer owned by white. Lotta the peoples meet up on a weekend. That particular night I think his wife were cookin'; he went in and this guy was gonna make him get out. That's what it started in that lil' store about. Him and the man got into it, and the man's son came 'n' broke 'em up. That gave 'em the best of Ed 'cause he couldn't handle both.

But then Ed had a couple of friends riding with him. One was Jack Fisher, a strong, big, dark man, built good. He ran in and got him a'loose. Ed ran to his car and got his rifle. This man came out to shoot, and he fired and killed him. That put Ed Noel on the run.

He went to a little store there at Brozville and told the lady he wanted some cartridges. Before he could get home with his wife and Jack Fisher 'n' 'em, he run up on Ed McGaw and Charles Pitchford's daddy. They car wouldn't crank. Ed got out with his gun, and they intended to push the car outta the road; but then two or three carloads of a Ku Klux Klan mob, a posse, drove up and just started shootin' 'cause they musta thought it was Ed's car.

Ed just stepped up on the bank with his loaded rifle. Those fellas just laid down in the car while holes was bein' shot all up in it. Then the sheriff and deputy drove up. I s'pose they was givin' the posse a chance to get the dirty work done by the time they got there.

And they asked was that nigger Ed Noel in there. They [McGaw and Pitchford] told him, "No sir." He had the flashlight on and saw Ed wasn't there. Then they went to Ed's car. The deputy had his pistol waving, and seem like he went to get Ed Noel's wife and pulled her.

That's when Ed started to poppin'. Put two bullets right in the back of the deputy's head. Then everyone started shooting. That's when the sheriff laid flat under the car shooting. Ed couldn't get him from the position he was in—up on the bank—so he shot the air out of that tire. The sheriff had to get on the short wave and call the ambulance.

When the ambulance was comin' in, Ed shot the lights out. And they carried the deputy back. They said he was named John Pat Malone. He knew he wasn't gonna live with them two bullets; they said they couldn't get a razor blade between them. And some of 'em say the she'ff was shooting at Ed and he the one killed Malone with a .38 ball, but the .22 the one that got him.

So Ed was able to skip on in the woods. They lightened up because it was raining 'n' sleeting. Ed went in a farmer's shed, where the sheep and the hay was, to keep warm.

That Sunday he was out at his house. They had whites up on the rooftop, scattered around the house. This guy was making his move up on the porch and when he pushed the door open—it's a two-door lil' ole shack—Ed hit him [shot him] upside the head, and he fell up in there. Then they just commenced to firin' on Ed. He lay down 'til they got through shooting, 'cause the holes was all in the house, just like a sifter when ya sifting the bread.

Ed had a pole he would hitch his horse to, and he put about three bullets in there. That's where he got one of the other whites. When he got out in the yard, he whirled, flipped the gun over his shoulder, and hit one on top of the house by the chimney. There was another by the car, and he shot that one.

One that was injured was Andrew Smith, who later became sheriff. All the rest of the whites threw their guns down and went a'fleeing for their life. Just one man, a black man, made five hundred whites move.

After Ed proceeded into the woods, they went after him with dogs from Parchman. They made Ed's brother go right behind the dogs so if Ed went to firing, he'd hit his brother. The dogs got close to him, but then the posse got jittery and went to shooting, which put the dogs off. Later, they gassed the house and set it afire.

They had airplanes to fly over, but he saw the airplane and put hisself in a stump position—he had been in the service. Then they got the National Guard, about five hundred of 'em. They couldn't find him, and he say he was looking right at them; he was up in a tree while they was combing the woods through and through, near shoulder to shoulder. He musta been in a hollow tree. They passed right by him.

By this time they were catching peoples walkin' to the stores and had little potted meat and wieners in the can, make 'em set on the ground for two or three hours trying to make 'em say they was carryin' Ed food.

They just harassed a lot of black people. Catch 'em out on the road, sit 'em down, dog 'em around, and call 'em names. They stopped me when I was riding with my cousin, who's kinda red-like and had kinda sandy hair. One guy had a 30–30 in this hand and a .45 on his hip. He was pointing his gun all up in my face, and the other one yanked on the door and pulled my cousin out. I tried to tell 'em that wadn't none of Eddie Noel. "Shut your mouth, nigger." They gave us a helluva time.

A lot of people, black peoples, had to stay at home. They couldn't travel freely, and it kind of upset 'em. It had the whites and blacks upset; 'cause I know I passed some whites' homes that they were nailin' wooden planks up over the windows and hanging sacks up so you couldn't see in. They was afraid and we was afraid. It just had the county in a turmoil, just shook the county—white and black.

Finally, they got the state people and the FBI to investigate. They come round through the country, got my daddy and a few others and say, "If he come here, cook him a good meal and tell him to give hisself up." They would guarantee to carry him to Jackson, where he would be safe and give him some treatment, and he would get a fair trial.

After a few weeks he turned himself in. They kept him in prison and Whitfield [the state hospital] for a while; then they sent him on North. He still in the North now, after he made five hundred guys drop their guns in the South.

What effect did the whole Eddie Noel thing have on blacks in Holmes County?

TC: It did give some of the black peoples the idea that they didn't have to take the beatin' and runnin' and that abusement like they had been. I've heard a lot of 'em say it was good that somebody had the courage and the nerve to stand tall like a man than be treated like an animal.

AUTHORS' NOTE: Mr. Johnson's account of the Eddie Noel incident is different from newspaper reports. The newspapers say that the original argument at

Dickard's store was between Dickard and a friend of Noel's. They say nothing of the McGaw and Pitchford car, nor do they detail the roadside gunfight apart from Noel's fatal shooting of Malone. The newspapers also put the number of men at Noel's house when Joseph N. Steward was fatally shot at far less than five hundred; some say as few as four men, but others imply that a large crowd had gathered.

However, the newspaper accounts of the incident are themselves contradictory, and all are based almost exclusively on the sheriff's account.

The Memphis *Commercial Appeal* confirms the local legend that Noel would shoot matches and cigarettes out of his wife's mouth with his .22 bolt action rifle.

MR. HENRY B. McCLELLAN

HOLMES COUNTY REGISTRAR

The Lexington Advertiser

"Principles and Men: Truth—the Weapon we use in their Defense."

128   Lexington, Mississippi—Thursday, September 30, 1965   Number Twenty-Seven

Will 'Blight Its Future' If It s C–R Laws, Says Sen. Stennis

ns Or Butter' y Be Choice In t Nam War

y W. F. MINOR
the New Orleans
Times-Picayune

John C. Stennis told nce of rural electric Columbia Saturday, Mis- would "blight its future" ks to defy federal laws vil rights field.

speaking to the an- ting of the Pearl River lectric Power Associa- h a segment of Negro embers in the audience,

we do not like some of which are being pressed our brow-laws which en passed in Congress undying and unyielding of your spokesmen in

nnis added: "Neverthe- are laws which were assed and enacted by the and they cannot be de-

Law And Order

ppi, the senator said, l must maintain a spirit and order. Any other ill take us downward eventually blight our

e portion of the 11,000 oup joined in the meet- under a circus tent in fair-like atmosphere, in- ntertainment by Minnie f "Grand Ole Opry"

hundred Negro mem- the rural electric asso- at as a group in the audience under the cir-

took issue with the Lyn- Johnson administration. "It is high time that Congress and the execu- nch realize that the war ry is not the only war

also commended the rural elec- tric groups. "Members of the electric power associations throughout Mississippi have made great contributions to the pro- gress of the state."

J. O. Cagle, manager of the Pearl River Valley Electric Power Association for the last 17 years, said in his report that the organization is conducting "the greatest system improvement pro- gram in the history" of the asso- ciation.

"This is your association — yours and your neighbors," he said.

"You can look forward to the future with confidence if you sincerely perform your respon- sibility as a member."

Included in the association are Marion, Lamar, parts of Law- rence, Jefferson Davis, Pearl River, Forest, Perry and Stone Counties.

Lions District Gov. To Speak Oct. 4th

Lion W. L. "Hoss" Peeler, Dis- trict Governor of Lions Inter- national of Kosciusko, will ad- dress the Lexington Lions Club on Monday night, October 4th, in the grammar school lunch room at 7:00 p. m., according to Lion Leo Alderman, club president.

President Alderman has issued an appeal to all Lexington Lions to be present early and greet Governor Peeler with the usual big smile and familiar Lexington welcome.

This will mark Governor Peeler's first visit to the Lexington club since his ele- vation to the highest position of Lionism in Mississippi at the state convention last June.

Governor Peeler is a native of Kosciusko and received his B.S. degree from Millsaps in 1929. Following graduation he entered the National Institute of Dry Cleaning in Silver Springs, Mary- land and after graduation enter-

Annual Homecoming At Antioch Baptist Church, October 3rd

On Sunday, October 3rd the members of Antioch Baptist Church, the neighbors and friends will gather in observance of the Annual Homecoming.

The Rev. Mack Massey of Glen Allen and a former pastor of the church will bring the Homecoming message at 11:00 o'clock.

The Rev. William Regal, pas- tor joins the church member- ship in a welcome to the public to attend.

Last Rites Held For William Word Monday, Sept. 27

Funeral services for William Word were held from the First Baptist Church, Indianola at 2 p. m. Monday, September 27th.

Young Word, 21 was killed in an automobile accident near Isola early Sunday morning. He was a lifelong resident of Indi- anola, a graduate of Indianola High School and had attended Mississippi State University.

At the time of his death he was groundman for Mississippi Power and Light Company, In- dianola and a member of the Baptist Church.

He leaves his parents, Mr. and Mrs. Fincher Word; two sisters, Sue Carroll Word and Louise Word; a brother, Robert Terry Word, and his maternal grand- mother, Mrs. John Carroll all of Indianola.

Federal Court Orders Holmes Registrar Not To Discriminate

Voter Applicants Previously Rejected Will Be Reexamined; New State Law To Be Basis Of Voter Qualifications

Discrimination against and discourtesies to Ne- gro voter applicants in Holmes County have been found by a Federal Court in a decision rendered Fri- day, September 24th.

Holmes County Circuit Clerk Henry McClellan has been ordered by a three-judge panel not to discrimi- nate against Negroes in registering voters, to determ- ine voter qualifications solely on the basis of new state laws, to examine all persons previously rejected and to handle all applications as quickly as possible.

Also, persons turned down by McClellan in the future will have the right to ask the court or a court-appointed examiner to re- view their cases.

At the same time the Federal court refused to waive the sim- ple literacy requirement still in effect under Mississippi state law. This has been widely hail- ed in the state press as a "vic- tory" for Mississippi's recent liberalization of voter require- ments. The state literacy re- quirement is still at odds with voting laws passed by Congress this year and it is still to be test- ed in the courts.

The ruling Friday came in a Justice Department suit filed against McClellan some time ago. Justice Department officials

had sought an order from the U. S. Court suspending all quali- fications for voting in Holmes County except basic ones involv- ing, age, residence, etc. They charged the Holmes Registrar with handling voter registration in a manner "which deprived Negro citizens of that county of the right to vote without distinc- tion of race and color."

The state argued that passage of new voting laws in Mississippi which have reduced heretofore stringent requirements for voting has rendered the case moot—but the Court said other discrimina- tory practices were charged to McClellan and supported by evi- dence. Negroes had been delayed in taking tests, while whites got

their tests the day they applied it continued. Discourtesies to Ne- groes were also spelled out.

The Court noted the new state laws had removed from state registrars discretionary powers which have been used in the past to discriminate against Negroes.

"A change of mind is clearly shown," the Court said regard- ing the situation in Holmes Coun- ty in recent days. (Several hun- dred Negroes have been register- ed this year, according to un- confirmed reports. Mr. McClellan stated Wednesday that he "did not know how many.")

When the suit was originally filed, Mississippi required po- litical voters to be able to read and interpret any section of the State Constitution to the satis- faction of the Registrar, to de- fine the duties of citizenship and be of good moral character — the Registrar being the sole determining authority — as well as ordinary requirements of age, residence, etc. State quali- cations today, because of pas- sage of the new laws in August, have been reduced to simple literacy.

Three-Judge Panel

The suit was heard by Circuit Judge Warren Jones of Florida, and District Judges Claude Clay- ton of Tupelo and Sidney Mize of Gulfport. When Judge Mize died before final arguments, Cir- cuit Judge Griffin Bell replaced him. Both sides waived rights at the time to a new trial.

State President

The Holmes Circuit Clerk was recently honored by the state association of circuit clerks in Mississippi when they elected him president.

Lexington Adopts

Tax Rate Remains The Same At 20 Mills; $188,965.00 Budget Set

The City of Lexington has adopted a $188,965.00 budget for the fiscal year 1965-66 and set the tax rate for the new year at twenty mills, eleven for bonds

"I Never Harassed Anybody"

KENNETH SALLIS & WILLA WILLIAMS

Since so many of the interviews in this book concern Mr. Henry McClellan, the circuit clerk during the 1960s, Kenneth Sallis sent him a letter explaining that we have interviewed many civil rights activists. The letter stated, "Many of them described how you harassed them when they tried to register to vote and you were the circuit clerk. We would like to interview you to get your side of the story."

Kenny called him two days later and was surprised when he agreed to be interviewed. We were nervous and a little scared as we walked up to the front door of his nice home. But he shook our hands, and that made us feel comfortable. Mr. McClellan is a thin elderly man who still looks healthy. He has white hair with large ears. His voice is deep but light; he speaks in a monotone. We took seats in his living room, and soon his wife, daughter, and grandson joined us.

We were disappointed when Mr. McClellan said we had to write down what he said instead of using a tape recorder. He also refused to sign the release form authorizing us to publish the interview. He told us that there was no use for the release form or the tape recorder because he was not going to say much anyway. Still, it was hard keeping up with his words. Willa wrote down all she could, and then we wrote the rest right after we left his house.

We had prepared an extensive interview guide, but we got only to a fraction of the topics before he told us that he was expecting company. We had really looked forward to asking him, "Why could you register only forty-eight blacks between June 1963 and the end of 1964, while federal examiners registered eighteen hundred and seven in five weeks in 1965?" Still, we appreciate Mr. McClellan's willingness to speak with us.

Mr. McClellan explained to us that he was elected circuit clerk of Holmes County in 1955. He served until 1980. Kenneth asked Mr. McClellan if any blacks had tried to register before April 9, 1963, when the first fourteen went up to the courthouse. He told us that no blacks had tried to register before that time, and that the first

fourteen came when court was in session and he was busy. He said
he was under oath, so he had to do what the law said. And the law
stated that before a person could register to vote, he or she had to
interpret a section of the Mississippi constitution, "which some of
them wouldn't even try to do." Mr. McClellan stated that he never
harassed anybody. "I gave them the paper and let them try."

He denied asking people how many bubbles are in a bar of soap or
how many hairs are on a donkey's back as part of the literacy test.
When we asked Mr. McClellan about having dogs at the courthouse
to discourage blacks from voting, he responded calmly, "Lies, lies,
absolutely lies. None of that was true." He admitted that some whites
who were registered could not read and write, but claimed that he
also helped some blacks register who were illiterate.

It surprised us that Mr. McClellan actually brought up the subject
of the lawsuit filed against him, the county, and the state of Mississippi by Robert Kennedy and the United States Department of Justice. A panel of three judges was appointed to judge the case. His
lawyers included Edwin White, Bill Allain, and Tom Watkins. The
case was tied up in court for two years. Mr. McClellan claimed that
he and the county won the case. But according to the *Holmes County
Herald*, the panel decided that "the evidence is such as not only per-
mits but requires a finding that the Registrar discriminated against
Negro applicants and favored white applicants."

We asked Mr. McClellan how the registration process changed
when the Voting Rights Act was passed. His wife told us that applicants no longer had to interpret sections of the Mississippi constitution. About the federal registrars who came to Holmes County later,
Mr. McClellan commented, "I wasn't the cause of them coming, and
I wasn't the cause of them leaving."

Mr. McClellan's daughter claimed that civil rights people made up
the stories of how her father had mistreated blacks. She said that these
people had their minds made up that if you were white, then you
were automatically against them.

Mr. McClellan explained that he owned a store in Cruger, Mississippi, before he was elected circuit clerk, and that 90 percent of his
customers were black. "Why would I treat them wrong?"

His daughter added that she could remember black people coming
into the store with no money. "Daddy would give them sacks and
sacks and sacks of food," she recalled with sentiment. "And if they
would have paid him back, he would never need anything."

MRS. LEOLA
BLACKMON

"I Couldn't Hold My Peace"

DWYANE BUCHANAN & JOHN DARJEAN

This interview and the interview
with Mr. William Eskridge are different from the rest because they
took place in Carroll County just north of Holmes County. Both
counties are rural, poor, and located on the edge of the Mississippi
Delta, but Carroll County's population is only 45 percent black. Also,
compared to Holmes County, very few blacks in Carroll County are
independent farmers who own their own land. The Movement in
Carroll County was never as strong as it was in Holmes County, and
it really only lasted for one year—1965.

During that year, however, a great deal happened, and Mrs. Leola
Blackmon was usually in the thick of it. Mrs. Blackmon is an intelligent, active, and courageous woman. She was one of the first people
to be involved in the Carroll County Movement, and she was the
only woman spokesperson. As you read this interview, you will learn
about split-session schools. You will also learn how Mrs. Blackmon lay
down with her children in front of the busses in Carroll County and
how, on that same day, she was jailed for assault when she jumped on
a deputy sheriff who had slapped her little son.

I hope her ability to remember past events in detail makes this
interview as interesting to read as it was to conduct. The interview
lasted one hundred minutes, so we had to cut a lot out—but not
before we had transcribed ninety-five pages!

We still have a long way to go in Holmes County before we
achieve racial justice, but Carroll County makes us appreciate what we
do have. Mrs. Blackmon told us that there are only three black elected
officials in Carroll County: coroner, election commissioner, and school
board member. White teachers in the public schools send their children to the private, all-white academies. Blacks still have almost no
voice in the way Carroll County is run.

[In the following interview, **LB** is Mrs. Leola Blackmon.]

&

Mrs. Blackmon, how did the Movement start in Carroll County?

LB: In 1964 we couldn't vote. So a few peoples from Carroll County started attending meetings with friends in Holmes County. We was able to bring [polling] boxes into Carroll County, and everybody on that Sunday before election day voted in our churches. And then all of these votes were compiled. The civil rights workers sent these numbers back to Washington to show how many peoples was left out of the election.

We started organizing when we got this civil rights worker, John Allen, from Rhode Island. About the beginning of 1965 we had our first meeting at Jeff Chapel C.M.E. Church. We organized the Freedom Democratic Party. That's who we worked through and got all our feedback from. There was a chairman in each district of the county, and we had the president of the whole county. We'd meet once a month in different areas of the county and make our reports to this countywide meeting. We didn't have nowhere to meet but our churches. On a Sunday evening, three to four o'clock, we'd have a church full of people from everywhere. We also would go to state meetings with Lawrence Guyot, the chairman of the state FDP, and Mrs. Fannie Lou Hamer.

We discussed issues, and from that we went to try to get everybody to register. They had this literacy test. They was mean about us coming into the courthouse. At times we would stand in line, and maybe in a run of a day, two or three would get a chance to take the test. And it went on for months. I'll say about April's when the first person passed the test. Every now and then somebody would pass. But it was something they didn't want us to do. They always tried to make the tests harder. And also we had to pay poll taxes. After we register, we have to pay a two-dollar poll tax in order to be able to vote.

Did the white people have to pay?

LB: They say they was paying, but we don't know because they was in charge of everything.

What about the literacy test? Did whites have to take that, too?

LB: I don't think they really had to take the test, and if they did, I'm sure they had help. When blacks was going to the courthouse, it would be a whole town of peoples watching. I think most of 'em was the Ku Klux Klan.

Were most black people at that time just watching and thinking y'all shouldn't have been doing that also?

LB: Most of the black people was afraid to get involved; they was afraid to even come into town and stand around.

Did they ever send federal people down to do registration in the post office?

LB: In 1965 they sent federal registration into Carroll County. They had a local office somewhere in the back of the post office. They didn't register in the courthouse.

When you brought your people up to register to vote, did the whites who were watching ever try to get back at them? Did the sheriff ever harass the people getting registered?

LB: Oh yeah. They even ran the car down. This woman, Jan, had a carload of peoples, and they shot into her car. They shot holes through the car when they left the courthouse. There's a long stretch on [Route] 35 with no houses or anything, and they tried to run her off the road.

That must've made it hard to convince people to register to vote.

LB: Yeah. And on May 11, 1965, we had a long line in Carrollton trying to register. They wouldn't let us stand in the hall. We lined up all the way from the circuit clerk's office on outside. And the white men rode around with their guns hanging up in their car. So we had peoples talk to the sheriff about these peoples riding around while we was standing in this line. And the sheriff said, "We can't keep them from riding around with those guns in the car. We don't have no authority to make them take those guns out." So some blacks just went home and got their trucks and came back with their guns.

We had a lot of harassments because we didn't have a place to meet. At one time everybody was afraid for us to meet in their church because they was burning down churches at that time. So we then built a little house down in Fletch Burt's field. That was our place of meeting. And you can go down there now and see bullet holes in that house where the people shot at us.

Were you ever there when they were shooting?

LB: I wasn't there at the time; I was on my way. But my momma and my daddy was there on that same night. They did strike the building with a few shots, but nobody got hurt. We had mens who guarded us, and they was standing out with high-power guns. They began to shoot back at this car, and they hit it. They say that car left there on a flat 'cause they shot the tires out. The laws didn't try to find out who did it.

Did the sheriff do anything to y'all men shooting back at them?

LB: No, they didn't bother us either. They just let everything go.

When we got so strong in the Movement, after we got our FDP organization going, there was a few of 'em that wasn't afraid of their harassments. They burned crosses in our yards just to make us afraid.

They burned a cross in houses like Percy Applewhite, Johnny Applewhite, Tanner Amos, L. C. Smith, and several others. They also burned a cross at my house.

We was living over in my mama's house, and we had just moved because the white peoples felt like we had got involved in the Civil Rights Movement. We had to move off of their land. So we moved here. We had nine children at the time. My husband was farming, and it was hard for us to borrow money from the bank. But the FmHA had to open up to blacks, and that's where we got our loan from.

After they found out we was in the Civil Rights Movement, they made things hard for us; they tried to make everything hard. The welfare department wouldn't even give us donated food. They'd say we was ineligible. So then I made a complaint to the Justice Department of the United States government. They sent somebody to investigate and sent the welfare supervisor along with him.

Were a lot of women involved at that time?

LB: When it began, we had a few womens who participated in our local meetings. But to go out and face the issues among the peoples, I was the onliest woman. Most times I was a spokesman for the group because most of them was nonparents of the schools. And after voter registration, we were working on the improvement of our schools.

Y'see, when they found out that we had mens who would resist the white mens, they began to calm down and started to negotiate with us and agree on issues. They come to me and told me all of my children could go to the white school.

And this I asked them: "If only my black childrens can go to your school and no other blacks, then I don't want mines in there either because my children got to grow up and they gonna want wives and husbands. You don't want them to marry your boys and girls. I'm not speaking for my children, I'm speaking for all black children of Carroll County." Then we filed this suit.

So you was one of the spokesmens at that point?

LB: Yes, most of the time I was one. The peoples was willing to follow me, but they wouldn't really be the main spokesman. But I had peoples to back me up, like Mr. Eskridge.

Could you tell us from the beginning how the whole school situation came about?

LB: We had split sessions for blacks only. They consolidated about sixteen little school shacks into one big school down to Blackhawk in 1956. And then they started busing the children to the school. They used two months in the summer for the black childrens to go to school and six months in the winter. The real hot months, our children was going to school. They didn't have cool water, no air conditioners, no fans. And when the children would come home, they would look like the road out there, they would be so dusty. And the childrens had to cram in that bus, about one hundred students.

Why did they have 'em going to school in the summer?

LB: They wanted the childrens to finish chopping, then they'd go to school. Then when they got out of school, they start picking cotton. So what aroused me and disgusted me, I felt like there wasn't anything we could do about it. Our children would start school in October and close in April. So one time there was so much cotton yet left in the field until the Board met, and they passed it that school wouldn't open 'til November. And when November came they said it was one woman—that woman lived in Holmes County, but her farm was in Carroll County—said she had so much cotton in the field that the children couldn't go to school until they got her cotton out of the field.

So that's when I questioned. I was living on a white man's farm, and I went to him and asked him, "Why is it that these are our childrens, and the white peoples on the Board are all white, and they makes schedules of when our children go to school and when they don't?"

And he pretend he didn't know anything. But I told him, I said, "Well, one of these days I'll find out." And from that day he began to tell the folks that I was a member of the NAACP.

Finally, he told my husband he wanted us to move off of his place because I was a member of the NAACP. Y'see, I never feared 'em, and that's what they couldn't understand. It was a big plantation of us, but I was the only one would stand up and tell them when I felt like this is wrong and I'm not going for it. Even my husband wanted to go along with everybody else, but I always disagreed. So we had to move here.

And it was around the Fourth of July. I met with these peoples in Jackson, and I was telling them about the split-session schools. They was working on integrating schools, not split session. So we went to Jackson to talk to 'em about our split-session school. But they gave me an address to write to this person in Washington; maybe we could get some help. So I wrote this letter. And I never got no answer.

So we continued to meet on these issues. Every time we would go to the school board, they would cuss the ones who we sent and threaten 'em not to come back. So we decided to block all the buses, not letting the buses go until we could get a big enough disturbment that we could hear from the federal government.

And this was the day that we blocked the buses, myself and my four childrens: One was eight, one was ten, one was eleven, and one fourteen.

We blocked this bus. And they couldn't get us to move. And they said they was gonna run over us. We still wouldn't move; we was just lying there. I laid the childrens all across the road just like a string, lined them up. And then I told 'em, "Now, don't nobody move. Let the bus come on over us." And they was strong enough to lie there. When we wouldn't move, these law officers was just taking us and piling us up on a pile. They put their bodies up on us to hold us to the ground so the bus could pass.

Those were law officers?

LB: Some of 'em were just deputized. And when we got over to the school hall, while the bus was loading, we surrounded this high school bus. And this little eight-year-old son of mine, he was on the front of the line. This big law officer which was deputized, he snatched him and slapped him. Slapped that little boy. That's what brought about a fight.

Did you jump on them?

LB: Yeah, we had a fight. There was two mens fighting me, and when they throwed me, they throwed me on my shoulder, and that knocked my shoulder out of place. Then they handcuffed me and took me to jail along with John Applewhite. They jailed him to get him out of the road from blocking the bus.

About how long did you stay in jail?

LB: I went to jail that morning about nine o'clock, and I was in there 'til after one. They gave me a dirty old mattress and told me I could lay on it if I wanted. So I laid down and went to sleep. I didn't know my arm was out of place. Before I knew anything, the FBI was calling me. When I'd gotten up, that's when I discovered there was something wrong with my arm.

Did the FBI help you?

LB: He just only asked me questions. And he asked the sheriff why I hadn't seen the doctor. I didn't lie—he didn't know I was hurt. So he called the doctor right quick and got an appointment to take me to the doctor at one.

Who was the sheriff then?

LB: Malcolm Bennett. And so when I went to the doctor, the sheriff was calling me to wake me up; he says, "Leola, Leola!" And this FBI says to him, "Will you call her Mrs. Blackmon? That is Mrs. Blackmon!" And the sheriff said "Mrs. Blackmon." And today, if I meet him, he still calls me "Mrs. Blackmon." I got an addition to my name that day!

And so he'd taken me to the doctor, and the doctor gave a report and everything, and the FBIs made pictures of my injuries. Afterwards, they had a hearing that same evening. They had got the state attorney and the judge. And they charged me with resisting arrest and disturbing the peace, assault on a law officer, and all that kinda stuff.

Couldn't you sue them?

LB: Well, I did.

Well, what happened that night?

LB: At this hearing, I had no lawyer at the time. John Allen was the only one to kind of represent me. And so when they gave all the charges and everything, then he had certified copies made of the charges so they couldn't change them. They said they couldn't give him copies, but he demanded he had certified copies of my charges, and they gave him certified copies of my charges. They charged him a big price for it, but he paid it and got them that day. Y'see, he knew what he was doing.

So they let me out on bond, and then the main hearing come up in about two weeks. And when the judge, the district attorney, everybody was there to try me, a federal attorney from Maryland turned around and told them who he was, and he was there to represent me. It looked like the whole courthouse, those white people was there, got excited. They looked like they didn't know what to do. He told them that he wanted to appeal it to the federal court. And then he turned around and asked me about suing, and we sued them for a hundred and fifteen thousand dollars.

Did they pay you?

LB: No, they dropped all the charges against me. We had peoples who were to testify for me. We had found out that they were gonna lie because they thought that I was gonna get a lotta money. They were my main witness, and they started to saying that they didn't see the man hit the child, and all that kinda stuff.

Your friends?

LB: My friends. People was saying I would be rich after getting $115,000. White peoples was telling 'em that I was gonna be the onliest rich black woman in Carroll County. And they began to believe it, and they got jealous. And so my attorney asked me, "What must I do?"

I said, "If they drop the case against me, let's drop it against them." See, if anybody ever been my friend, Malcolm Bennett have been my friend. He have been a lot of help to me. And he always shows great respect.

So what happened with that whole education issue after they put you in jail?

LB: On the same day they had me in jail, almost everybody in Carroll County was marching around the town of Carrollton. A lot of peoples that never had been a part of the Movement, that was a day a lot of them stepped in, even cheering. Parents wouldn't let their children get in; they wanted to be a part, but they wouldn't let them in. 'Cause I had a cousin up the road, she said when her children got home that day they were so wet and sweaty, and they say, "Mr. Percy Lee is coming by in his truck, and we goin' to Carrollton."

She said, "No, you ain't goin' to no Carrollton."

They told her, "Yessir, we're goin' to Carrollton this evenin'; we don't care if you don't ever go. We are goin'!" And she just didn't say anything else. When Percy went by with that pickup truck, they just loaded on.

L. C. Smith was the leader, and he was singing, "Wasn't nobody gonna turn him around." This man who was working for the city of Carrollton said when L. C. went 'round town singing with all of them peoples behind him, he said he throwed his tools down and got in the march. That's what really brought more peoples in. They gave us a Mason hall in Carrollton for a meeting place. The Ku Klux Klan burned it down. Then we built this little center over to Vaiden.

But that morning we was blocking the buses; we had a few people blocking 'em all over the county. We didn't have everybody involved, but at that moment we brought more peoples in. We was really close together. Well, that same day they stopped the split-session school. It haven't been split sessions since.

But, see, I put in my letter [to Washington] that it was only a school with children and teachers, no textbooks. All the textbooks was outdated. The white kids got all new books. They put the old books in this school. When federal attorneys along with the school board went to investigate, this school board member said when they opened up one of those books and he saw that the books was from this other school, he say he almost fainted. He said he had to beg my pardon. He thought I was lying. See, every time you think a group is dirty, everybody in that group is not dirty. He said he were ready to go to federal court himself, right then. He said they really had appropriated that money for the school books. I said, "Y'know, it's a lot goin' on; you really don't know what you're doing yourself."

So that same school term, they integrated in September. They only integrated first through third and the twelfth grade in the white schools so's blacks could go there. And my oldest son was in twelfth grade, and he was looking forward to major in math. He never had civics or a business course. They didn't even have 'em in the black schools. But, after all, he wanted to stay on in the black school because he was the president of his class. He was an A-student, and he went on to college.

I had three to go to the white school. We only had six blacks to go that first year. There was a few more pulled in the next year. We also integrated eleventh grade the next year.

What was it like to send the kids, and what happened to them?

LB: These first six, three were mines, two was Johnny Applewhite's, and one was L. C. Smith's. Everybody was very nice to them. I guess the parents was teaching the other children, "Just let 'em have the swings and all the play equipment on the campus." So they did real good the first year; the teachers was nice to 'em and everything.

What about the students?

LB: They didn't do much playing with 'em. But just this last year this one white kid—he's grown now—told my husband he was in school with my two younger boys. He said when they came to school, he was so happy, and he would play with them. Said they would wrastle, and they had the biggest time. His sister told his mama he was "playing with them niggers." Say his mother whooped him. Afterward, they put him in private school. See, it was not the children; it was the adults.

When did the adults pull their children out and take them into the private schools?

LB: When we integrated the whole school—junior high and high school. My daughter had a lot of white friends in the seventh grade, but they just kept pulling her friends out one by one until she got all the way up in high school. I don't think more than one or two of the white girls that was her classmates graduated with her. And then at graduation time—up until this last year in Vaiden—the whites would graduate, but they wouldn't march in the graduation ceremony. It would be a very few whites.

Why didn't they go to the academy?

LB: I guess they was too poor. But like one guy, his family was rich. But he went to school all the way through with the black children. I guess his family thought it was right. But he didn't march with them in the graduation activity—that was the only thing he didn't do. I guess his friends and everybody maybe harassed him about graduating with black kids.

When did y'all get Head Start?

LB: That was in 1966. I just tell the truth—when Head Start got into the county, that split up everything.

How's that?

LB: When they got the pre-schools in Carroll County, our leaders all jumped out of our organizations, our Freedom Democratic Party, and went for those jobs. That left the peoples that were following. Y'know how that is when something happen to a leader and nobody else can really just go on. They had peoples to take over, but didn't have nobody strong enough to know the issues and follow them up. I stayed with the programs longer than anybody else. All these leaders in the county jumped off. If they didn't take a job, their wife took a job.

The Movement began to get weak. Then those poor peoples who had all interest in these leaders, they started saying, "They using us to get everything for themselves!" Which it was true. It was sure enough true. It was like I said: It was weak peoples in Carroll County. They were and still is satisfied.

Finally, it was a job opening, and they kept begging me to take the job—I did need a job—so I take the job as teacher.

Are you satisfied?

LB: NO!

What still needs changing?

LB: Schools. It's in a bad predicament, worse than when my children was there. The curriculum is just rotten. The principal of this school, his children went to the private academy. And teachers in our school, their children's in the academy. The school board is all white, except one black woman just got on there.

What else needs changing in Carroll County?

LB: The banks, the courthouse. Nobody black work in no bank in Carroll County. Nobody black work in the courthouse in Carroll County. Circuit court's office, chancery court office—ain't nobody in those offices but white peoples. Blacks work in the justice court—secretaries—but you know that ain't nothing. They just not gonna hire black peoples. Not a single black works in the office of the superintendent of education. They just work as teachers, janitors, and bus drivers.

Far as jobs in Carroll County, everything needs changing. Black peoples are still children in Carroll County. They got black law officers—they gotta have blacks there. Even the chief of police in Vaiden is black. But as far as the business part of the county, there's no blacks. Blacks work for the whites, but it's not very many black businesses in Carroll County.

Then the whites don't have to have a degree to do anything here. But blacks can have a degree and can't do it. The board of supervisors is all white, and the black folks here is not gonna vote for nobody black. 'Cause we had a chance to put black folks on—twice. Ain't no use in telling them, "He gave you the money. Now, still vote for your color, for your race." All that white man's gotta have is a few dollars. My people's just too satisfied.

It's just a good handful who really continue to stick together and try to do things in Carroll County. We had a great NAACP organization in the county. It's so little now, ain't very much we can do with it. It just the same little handful meet on any issues. At one time blacks was together in Carroll County, and we made a lotta progress. But right now, it look like it's failing. It seem like because of the noninterest of the younger peoples. The main ones we need to be involved are from twenty-two to thirty-five.

Why do you think most of the people dropped out from the meetings?

LB: They lost confidence in their leaders. It looked like the peoples stopped teaching our childrens about issues. I had a man tell me that they ought not to come up with this mess about Martin Luther King's birthday—a black man.

Going back to when y'all protested, where did you travel to?

LB: We was mostly involved in the state marches like the James Meredith march from Memphis to Jackson.

Could you tell us a little about that?

LB: Yes, he got shot. When he got to Vaiden, that's where we had a big meeting. We pulled a lot of peoples into the Movement after he had got shot. When he got back on the road to start back marching, after he was shot, he was almost in Vaiden. Everybody wanted to see him, and peoples went and got in the march, just to get a chance to see him. We had a meeting at the church that night, and his feets were just red from where he had been walking, and he even showed his bruises where he was shot. It looked like he touched the peoples. Peoples who had never taken part in it got involved. The marching went on into Jackson. My mama and daddy, both's old, but they walked from Tougaloo to Jackson.

Did they ever try to stop the march?

LB: No more than they shot James Meredith in the march. That was at Senatobia, Mississippi. But even while he went in the hospital, the march kept on; they kept walking.

And we marched around Winona Hospital at the time they beat Miss Fannie Lou Hamer. She got off the bus up there, and they beat her up and put her in jail. She had went to drink water in the white part of the waiting room. They beat her up there in Winona, in the jailhouse. That's when people from all over the state marched around. It was just a trying time. It's just how mean the people were. You hadda be somebody to stand up. Lotta peoples were willing, but they were fearful.

How did you overcome your fear?

LB: I tell you the truth: I never had no fear. I guess I had too much of my grandaddy in me. My grandaddy hated white peoples. I never been to the point that I really didn't like white peoples, but I just didn't never fear them. It was always brought up to me—I don't supposed to fear peoples. But one thing I learned young and that's everything possible through Jesus Christ. I don't feel like I oughta have feared mens. The one I feared's Jesus Christ.

That night when they set that cross afire at my house, I didn't notice it was a cross until they threw the match. I thought to cut 'em down, but I didn't. I just let some bullets through behind 'em. I had a rifle. It would shoot sixteen times, and I just lit out up there and started shooting.

Did most people have a gun at home, and were they prepared to use it?

LB: Yeah, all of us that was involved.

How did that work with what Dr. Martin Luther King was saying about how the Movement was nonviolent?

LB: Well, we said nonviolent when we was protesting the school buses; nobody not s'posed to fight. But that fight was brought on because we were looking for them to hit *us*. And we had got prepared to accept that. But we never thought about them gonna hit our little children. When he slapped that child, I couldn't hold my peace then. 'Cause he didn't know why that man slapped him, and nobody else didn't get slapped. He'll never forget it, even though he were eight years old.

My mama didn't want me to go no place. And my husband was afraid—he weren't going nowhere but home. I always had Percy, Tanner Amos, and John Applewhite—those were my buddies. We went with a old raggly car. One time it didn't even have a floor in it, and it would be so cold. Sometime we had to get out and work on those cars and then go. Be all hours of the night.

Were you afraid that your family might get hurt by the Klan?

LB: Well, no, my mama was more afraid about 'em than anybody. But I ain't ever believed they was gonna get up to my house. That night I was watching, but if my husband hadn't been riding that night, they never woulda stayed out there and put that cross down.

Did the Citizens' Council foreclose on anybody's mortgages?

LB: They mostly didn't foreclose on nobody here in Carroll County, but they wouldn't give 'em any more loans. They tried to be self-sufficient, started buying cotton pickers, so peoples didn't have to pick cotton for 'em no more—all they could do to keep money out of black people's hands. But Carroll County is small, and once they found out they couldn't make it without black peoples, they began to get friendlier. They saw they couldn't live without us, as it was hard for us to live without them.

Did the Klan do anything else here in Carroll County to discourage y'all?

LB: Only thing the Klansmen did was burned the crosses, that we know. They would ride around with their guns, trying to frighten us. But let's tell the truth: It's hard to frighten Blackhawk folks.

Did they ever come out in public and say anything?

LB: No, never in public. They'd do it sneaky.

The cross burnings, the people shooting in the meetings and striking children— where did that hate come from?

LB: When we was growing up, we had white childrens lived next door. Those white parents would go off, and their children'd stay at our house with my mama, just like the black children. Those white children have slept in our house, have ate in our house. But this very white man, our next-door neighbor, after this Movement came about, he could almost walk into you and wouldn't speak. And I been around him all my life. Seems like they say: "This is ours, and we don't want nobody to have it." They wanted us all to be always like little childrens and have to take what they give us.

When we was children, it was just as many whites lived around us as blacks. Black and white children played together, and we'd eat at each other house. I can't understand how that hate came about.

MR. WILLIAM B. ESKRIDGE

"We Still Got a Long Ways to Go"

DWYANE BUCHANAN, JOHN DARJEAN,
& JAY MACLEOD

Mr. William Eskridge was the second person we interviewed from Carroll County. Mrs. Leola Blackmon told us that people respect his opinion and look upon him as a source of great wisdom. Right after interviewing Mrs. Blackmon, we went with her to Mr. Eskridge's house outside of Carrollton. We were feeling a little tired after our first interview, and the sticky August heat was pressing on us. We conducted the interview with Mr. Eskridge outside in his carport.

On meeting Mr. William Eskridge, you would never guess his age. Even back in the '60s, Mr. Eskridge was an elderly person. We still find it hard to believe that he is eighty-nine years old. His features are so young and sprightly. He is a short, slim man with a friendly smile. He made us feel comfortable right away.

Mr. Eskridge was wearing good old-fashioned lace-up boots. He leaned forward as he talked to us, and when he described something exciting, a glint would appear in his eyes.

Mr. Eskridge actually registered to vote in the 1920s. He remembered going down to the Black and Tan Republican state convention in 1928. The party was headed up by Perry Howard, a black lawyer born in Ebenezer in our home county of Holmes.

Mr. Eskridge also related the brutal lynching in neighboring Montgomery County in 1937. Roosevelt Townes and "Bootjack" McDaniels, two black men accused of killing a white merchant, were abducted by a mob in broad daylight as they came out of the courthouse. The mob lashed them to two pine trees and burned them up with blow torches.

Because we were so busy with the Leola Blackmon interview, Jay actually did much of the editing of Mr. Eskridge's interview. We hope you enjoy reading his words as much as we enjoyed hearing them.

[In the following interview, the speakers are Mr. William B. Eskridge (**WE**) and Mrs. Leola Blackmon (**LB**).]

↘

Could you tell us about your role in the Civil Rights Movement here in Carroll County?

WE: I been in the Civil Rights Movement way back yonder when we were tryin' our best to get people registered to vote. That was in 1928. I went to the state convention in Jackson. Perry Howard was the main leader of the party. Now, he was a Republican. The only way we could get in politics at that time was through the Republicans, because the Democrats called themselves lily-white. You couldn't get in there.

We got about fourteen or fifteen people in the Movement. Eventually, we got that many registered, too. So we decided we'd get a group and go vote in 1932. I was teaching school in Carrollton. The day came for voting; I went to the poll in Carrollton. They didn't want me to have a ballot. I stood there a while and went back up and told them, "I got to have a ballot." They gave me a ballot, and I voted that time.

One man went to McCarley, but the white people told him, "Uncle, you're qualified, but we advise you not to go." And those who were to follow me in Carrollton didn't. So you had one man voted, and you know what position it threw me in.

One of the school board members told me when I went back to get another contract to teach school for another year, he said, "If I hear of you teachin' politics in that school, we gon' put you out the next day."

I looked at him and said, "I'm not down there to teach politics, but I do teach civics, and whatever come up in civics, I'm teachin' it" [chuckles]. At that time you had to have a way around them. You just couldn't come out the way we do today. So I got over that hurdle.

I voted once or twice more in the general election. I went to the polls one time, and they didn't want to give me a ballot. We had a lawyer here—mighty fine man, Mr. Ewell—and they asked him was I qualified. "Yeah, Eskridge's qualified." So that settled that.

After that, I had to quit politics. My reason for quittin' was if I couldn't get enough folks to follow me, I wasn't doin' anything but hurtin' myself. I knew I would soon be in a place where I wouldn't have a job. So I pulled back and didn't vote anymore until the '60s.

I believe the first time I got in the real Civil Rights Movement in the '60s, I went to Jeff Chapel to the first meeting. John Allen, a white civil rights worker from Rhode Island, was there. Mrs. Blackmon was chairman that night. I went there to help out, but before I left there, they had made me president of the whole thing. Consequently, I had to go to work.

From then on, we had quite a few meetings, quite a few run-ins and so forth. Because white people don't take things in our county like they should. They had the opinion that we should accept whatever they say. Of course, I couldn't blame them much because we had been mostly acceptin' of whatever they said.

But when John Allen got here, he was able to get some black peoples that would stand up for what they felt was right. Don't think we had many that was able to stand up. The main ones we had was Mrs. Blackmon and L. C. Smith. There was a few more, but they wasn't as brave as L. C. Smith. We had another one known as Lynn Collin, who was about the bravest one we had in the whole pack. He didn't mind standin' up against them.

My main role was to try to guide the thing in order to keep down as much violence as we could. Some places had quite a bit of violence. We did have a little in Carroll County. Reason we didn't have but a very little is because whenever anything come up, they generally sent me ahead to see could we smooth it out. After living in the county since 1900, I was older than most of the people here that was in these movements. I was able to meet with people, talk with them, and smooth things out.

They had a march on Carrollton, and that march did more good than anything else because it put those people on notice that black people in Carroll County were not afraid. They didn't mind goin' up against a lot of things. So I went first to talk to the chancery clerk and the sheriff. I told them what we was plannin'. 'Course I know they didn't like it, but still they had to accept it.

We went to Carrollton one day to register people to vote. Mrs. Blackmon was there that time, and so was John Allen and a few more that the sheriff wanted to put in jail. He told me he gonna put them in jail if they keep on like they goin'. I told him, "You're the sheriff; I can't tell you what to do, but one thing: It may be better if you don't."

He didn't arrest them. I knew what was gon' happen if he arrested them. We'd've been on that courthouse like fire. We stayed around that courthouse all day long, and didn't a single person register.

Why weren't they able to be registered?

WE: Because they didn't want black folks to register. It was against their religion.

LB: A few got a chance to try the test, but nobody passed.

The literacy test?

LB: Right. Nobody passed the literacy test.

Way back when you voted in the '30s, had they made you pay the poll taxes?

WE: Yes, we had to pay the poll tax. That literacy test came later, but the poll tax came on way back yonder before '32, back yonder when my father was comin' on. They figured that black people didn't have the money—they didn't have the money—to pay poll tax. Most of us at that time worked for around fifty cents a day. Women cooked for white people every day for two dollars a week. Because one thing you can do, you can take the money away from black people and they can't survive. The whites knew that.

What used to be the biggest landowner in this county had a big store up in Carrollton, and my daddy heard him telling a white feller: "One thing we do, we give that Negro fifty cents a day. You keep him down by keepin' the money out of his hand." And that's what they did. I taught school for one dollar and something a day. Now, you can't get nowhere on that kind of money.

So when they had the poll tax back then, two dollars was a whole lot of money?

WE: That was a lot of money. And the black folks couldn't pay that.

Later on they had to find another way to keep black folks from voting; that's when they put on literacy tests?

WE: Right. Now, let's come up to another situation. We tried to get a high school in Carroll County. They did not want us to have one. We had little schools all over the county. We finally got the agricultural high school in 1938 at the small community school in Summerfield. There was no transportation. The small school building was turned into a girls' dormitory; the attic of the school building was made for the boys. The only way a child could go to high school was to go there and board.

There wasn't no bus?

WE: I didn't have any money, but I was tryin' my best to help out when that school started in '38. They didn't have a way to get there, and I got that truck and made a bed on it and hauled children myself.

LB: The only high school we had in 1954 was this Summerfield, and then they started busing. A bus run from Blackhawk and one run from Carrollton. Everybody had to get their children to this one route—no matter where your house was.

WE: Then we tried our best to get eight-months' school, and they wouldn't do no way to give it. My children were goin' to school right up here in Ebenezer [in Carroll County], a little bitty school. I went and asked the superintendent for eight months schooling for my children. That man shook his head: "No, we can't do it."

I listened as long as he up in the air. When he came back to the ground, I coolly said "Mr. So-and-so, my children gotta have eight months school."

Then he wanna know how close my children stay to Summerfield. He were gonna see maybe he could make arrangements to get my children to Summerfield. He wanted to satisfy me and let the rest go. If he put mines down there, that wasn't going to satisfy me because I was still going to wait until all of them get it.

So we went to Oxford to file a suit in the federal court. We had the best civil rights lawyer in the country, John Rosenberg. I remember before I went to Oxford, a school board member says to me, "Hmmm. Court order in the letter. See what you got me in. I don't like it a bit. I just don't want you carryin' me to court."

I said, "Sir, any time the federal government ask me a question, I gotta tell the truth. If tellin' the truth caused you to be offended, I'm sorry" [chuckles].

So the people in Carroll County decided they didn't want split sessions where our children didn't have but six months of school. They made our children go to school two months in the hot summer time so they could pick the white people's cotton [in the late autumn].

Mrs. Blackmon and John Allen and a few more went to different places and laid down in front of those school buses to keep 'em from runnin'. They couldn't do a thing but get the sheriff.

The sheriff came out; thought he could handle things. And Mrs. Blackmon messed around there and got in a fight [laughs]. I believe one of the sheriff's deputies tried to jump on her, and she [chuckles] gave him a good round [all laugh].

Now, that's the thing. You got to have people what have *guts*. Plus common sense. You got to have them both. Because if you have all guts and no common sense, you'll mess up things. We tried to keep our best people in front, so we couldn't mess up. We coulda messed around here and got two or three dozen people killed in a place like Carroll County.

Was it in 1937 when two black men were lynched?

WE: That was in Montgomery County. They had two fellers in jail in Winona that killed a white man. And the mob group came to the jail and got the men out. Now, you know they had to have some help with the jailer and the sheriff and so forth. The mob carried the two of them from Winona to Duck Hill. And that's where they blow-torched them to death. They blow-torched those poor boys; and one thing about it, Winona has been going down ever since. Today it's in bad shape.

Montgomery County's like Carroll County. Carroll County had lynchings in the 1800s. People had to jump out of the courthouse window up there. Her granddaddy [nodding to his wife] jumped out of the courthouse window there in Carrollton from a lynch mob. He happened to make it, but they killed quite a few of them. While court was settin', they came up on horses with their guns and started shootin' and killed quite a few. Now that was in the 1880s, I think. This is hearsay, what I heard when I was coming up; I didn't see it myself.

And another mob in Carroll County in 1901 killed a boy, so I was told. I was born in 1900. Some peoples lived right across here on your left. They killed those peoples' son because my father had to go get his coffin. See, some white boys' mama and papa came up killed; they were slaughtered.

Now, those boys said this black boy killed them. They wanted to kill all the blacks in a ten-mile-square area. That's what they wanted to do. They lynched the boy, and they killed that boy's mama and his sister. When they hung that girl from the tree, her baby was born. Those people lived right across the hill in the place adjoining mine.

After that the white peoples got together and stopped this ten-mile-square, but they didn't do nothin' to those boys. Eventually, they found out why their mother and father got killed. They could have found out at the start, but they didn't try. Those boys killed their mother and father for the insurance. Now Carrollton hasn't got anywhere since then. Instead of goin' up, Carrollton is going down. That's just my opinion.

How did they kill that first boy?

WE: He was down here at the bridge tying up horses, and they came down and just shot him. Now all the things that happened in Carroll County were enough to make anybody not want to be in the Movement.

Now, one thing about it, there have always been just a few black people going to speak up; the rest of them gonna drag. Nine cases out of ten, they gonna carry the news back to the white man. Because when I was in the Civil Rights Movement, we had two or three fellers that followed us in order to carry the news back. I always told them, "I'd rather you let me tell the white man, myself. But if you gotta tell him, be sure you tell him just what I said." Any time we had a meeting, they had those people there waitin' to carry the news back.

You knew who they were?

WE: Oh yeah, I knowed them well. I'm still friendly with 'em [chuckles]. Yeah, let them carry it; it doesn't matter. I would've welcomed any white person to come to our meeting. I'd tell him, "All right, have a seat!" We weren't doing anything undercover.

Who did the civil rights workers stay with?

WE: They lived with blacks.

Did the local whites ever try and do anything to them?

WE: They wanted to, but. . . .

LB: The local peoples didn't bother 'em because it's one thing about local whites: They'll do things sneaky, but they won't meet you face to face and try anything.

WE: Now, they wanted to try their best and get some black people to do something to them.

LB: That's right. They'd rather put the black person up to it. We had some blacks pick at us, too. I had a cousin, he stayed next door to me. He really did get hypnotized.

WE: Look like some of our peoples didn't want the Movement. They were brainwashed. You can easily brainwash a person if he doesn't have any sense. We got a long way to go with our own people.

But one thing I say, these whites really ain't that different today from what they was yesterday. The white peoples are still white peoples. And we still got a long ways to go. . . .

All: Amen!

CHRONOLOGY OF EVENTS
The Holmes County and
National Movements, 1963–1967

1963

March: At the invitation of Mileston farmers, SNCC begins work in Holmes County.

April: Approximately 14 blacks from Mileston attempt to register to vote.

May: Hartman Turnbow's home shot into and firebombed. He and 4 civil rights workers arrested for arson.

U.S. Justice Department files lawsuit against sheriff for intimidating potential black voters.

Birmingham campaign led by Dr. King's Southern Christian Leadership Conference (SCLC) reaches its climax as 959 children are arrested.

June: Black veteran killed by Lexington police.

Medgar Evers assassinated in Jackson.

July: Black youth killed by town marshall in Tchula.

Aug: Dr. King delivers his "I Have a Dream" speech at March on Washington.

Sept: 4 black girls killed in Birmingham church bombing.

Holmes County activists travel out of state to citizenship training workshops sponsored by SCLC.

Nov: 80,000 black Mississippians, Holmes Countians among them, cast ballots in mock "freedom vote."

President John F. Kennedy assassinated.

1964

Jan: 24th Amendment eliminates poll tax on federal elections.

Feb: Trial of Byron de la Beckwith for the murder of Medgar Evers ends in a mistrial.

Federal judge rules against Holmes County sheriff but decides that injunction is unnecessary.

Mississippi Freedom Democratic Party (MFDP) formed.

June: Holmes County blacks try to attend Democratic Party precinct meetings. Turned away, they elect their own delegates to MFDP state convention.

3 civil rights workers—Chaney, Goodman, and Schwerner—disappear in Neshoba County.

33 volunteers, mostly northern white students, come to Holmes County as part of freedom summer. They help with political organizing and teach literacy, voter education, and black history in "freedom schools."

Whites step up harassment. Both blacks and whites are heavily armed.

July: President Johnson signs Civil Rights Bill.

Local white arrested for assaulting white civil rights worker in front of courthouse.

Civil rights workers' car burned in Mileston.

Aug: Bodies of Chaney, Goodman, and Schwerner found under 20 feet of clay in an earthen dam.

By summer's end, over 1,500 blacks are "freedom registered" in Holmes County. But almost all who try to register at the courthouse are rejected.

3 federal judges appointed to hear lawsuit filed by Justice Department against Holmes County circuit clerk.

25 Holmes Countians attend state MFDP convention. Hartman Turnbow is elected as one of the delegates to the national Democratic convention.

After attempted dynamiting of Mileston church, armed guards are posted at homes and churches.

Home near Tchula firebombed.

Office of Economic Opportunity created to administer federal anti-poverty program.

MFDP's challenge to the seating of the regular Mississippi delegation at the national convention in Atlantic City, N.J., draws national attention.

Sept: Holmes County civil rights workers jailed on traffic and vagrancy charges. They each receive $250 fines and 60 days on the county farm.

Oct: Turnbow's home hit by 4 shots.

Nov: Over 2,500 Holmes Countians mark "freedom ballots" for the MFDP slate in mock election.

Scores testify in suit against circuit clerk about delays and discourtesies while trying to register.

Dec: Wilburn Hooker, state representative from Lexington, re-elected state director of Citizens' Council.

1965

Jan: 40 Holmes Countians travel to Washington, D.C. to support MFDP challenge of the newly-elected Mississippi congressional delegation. 600 witnesses give 10,000 pages of testimony before the House.

Holmes County Board of Education notified that it has until March to sign pledge of compliance with new civil rights laws.

Feb: Malcolm X assassinated.

Integrated groups test two libraries in Holmes County.

March: Eighty marchers are injured by lawmen as they attempt to cross the Pettus Bridge in Selma, Alabama. Three die in the Selma campaign.

April: Holmes County School Board receives two petitions—one representing 467 black parents, the other representing 445 students from Lexington and Tchula Attendance Centers concerning pledge.

June: 500 march in Lexington in support of MFDP and black voting rights in Holmes County.

120 blacks integrate Durant State Park.

July: Head Start opens in Lexington followed by 4 other Head Start centers in active communities.

200 Holmes Countians join freedom march in Jackson where over 100 Holmes Countians are arrested and jailed at the state fairgrounds. Two from the county are beaten badly and charge police brutality on national television.

Mississippi legislature drops from the books many provisions that block black voter registration. Registration in Holmes County begins to pick up.

NAACP attorneys file desegregation suit against Holmes County.

Judge Harold Cox orders Holmes schools to desegregate four grades each year.

Aug: President Johnson signs the Voting Rights Act of 1965, eliminating literacy requirements and allowing federal examiners to register black voters in some southern counties.

Insurrection in Watts section of Los Angeles is worst race riot in U.S. history.

Sept: 187 Holmes County blacks (highest in the state) enroll in grades 1–4 in formerly all-white schools.

All white children withdraw from desegregated grades in Lexington and Tchula. Some whites continue to attend Durant Public School but soon leave.

Private academies set up by whites.

Nightriders attempt to set Second Pilgrim Rest Church afire.

Gun battle between nightriders and armed guards takes place at community center in Pilgrim Rest.

Crosses burned in Durant, including at the cleaning plant of Mayor C. H. Blanton who reportedly encouraged white parents to keep their children in desegregated classes.

NAACP files suit against School Board for using state funds for private academies.

Federal court finally rules that Henry McClellan discriminated against black voter applicants.

More blacks are registered, but not enough. Holmes County FDP sends off more affidavits to the Justice Department charging continued discrimination by circuit clerk.

$1500 raised to send another busload to Washington to support MFDP challenge.

Holmes County activists fight new state law requiring tuition payments for students with parents residing out of state. Law prevents 500 Holmes Countians from enrolling in school. 15-year-old Willie E. Carthan of Tchula is the leading plaintiff in suit filed against State Board of Education.

Oct: Durant listed among 67 KKK Klaverns by House Un-American Activities Committee.

"Nocturnal Messenger" distributed around county to threaten blacks and white moderates.

Nov: Mrs. Lillie Mae Howard shot by nightriders in her home. Cooper Howard returns fire and is later arrested.

3 federal examiners begin voter registration in post offices.

Blacks elected in farm elections.

Dec: Whites print poster listing names of black parents sending their children to formerly white schools in Durant.

KKK parades through Tchula, Lexington, Acona, Mount Olive, and other Holmes County communities.

Black voter registration hits 2,500, of which 1,807 were registered since federal registrars arrived.

Blacks begin selective buying campaign to protest white boycott of public schools, segregated facilities, police brutality, fear of voting, and other grievances.

1966

Jan: Crosses burned at homes of children attending integrated schools.

KKK threatens to kill Hazel Brannon Smith.

Dr. King launches campaign in Chicago.

Feb: A few Holmes Countians join sharecroppers in their occupation of Greenville air base.

Black activists begin struggle to maintain control over Head Start funds as whites lead formation of Community Action Program.

March: Lawsuit filed against Holmes County Community Hospital citing discrimination and segregated facilities.

June: James Meredith is wounded by a white sniper as he marches from Memphis to Jackson. The march is continued by civil rights leaders. Originally scheduled to pass through Holmes County, the march detours through Delta counties. SNCC's Stokely Carmichael first uses the slogan "black power." Many Holmes Countians are among those beaten and teargassed in Canton. The march ends in Jackson with a rally of 30,000 people.

Black voter registration in Holmes County tops 5,000.

Grades 1–7 and 12 are ordered desegregated.

July: Riots break out in Chicago and Cleveland.

Aug: 35 white children return to public schools.

Oct: The Black Panther Party is formed in Oakland, CA.

Dec: SNCC decides to exclude whites from membership.

1967

March: Campaign begins in Durant to integrate restaurants and all public facilities.

April: FDP announces it will run a slate of candidates in county elections.

June: Riots in Boston begin summer of riots in U.S.

July: Judge orders full integration of Holmes County schools, and all whites leave all grades for academies.

Oct: Suit filed in federal court against all Holmes County law enforcement agencies for over 20 cases of alleged assault and battery.

Nov: Robert Clark first black to be elected to state legislature since Reconstruction.

ACRONYMS

CAP Community Action Program

CDGM Child Development Group of Mississippi

C.M.E. Colored Methodist Episcopal

CMI Central Mississippi Incorporated

COFO Council of Federated Organizations

CORE Congress of Racial Equality

FBI Federal Bureau of Investigation

FDP [Mississippi] Freedom Democratic Party

FmHA Farmers' Home Administration

GCA Greenwood Credit Association

LES Lexington Elementary School

MFDP Mississippi Freedom Democratic Party

NAACP National Association for the Advancement of Colored People

ROCC Rural Organizing and Cultural Center

SCLC Southern Christian Leadership Conference

SNCC Student Nonviolent Coordinating Committee